LITTLE HOUSE ON THE FREEWAY

In appreciation for your support of Focus on the Family, please accept this copy of *Little House on the Freeway* by Tim Kimmel. Your contributions enable this organization to address the needs of homes through radio, television, literature and counseling.

We trust the information on the following pages will enable you to find peace in the midst of a hurried schedule, and help restore inner contentment for all areas of your life. We know this book will make a fine addition to your home library.

Focus on the Family
Pomona, CA 91799

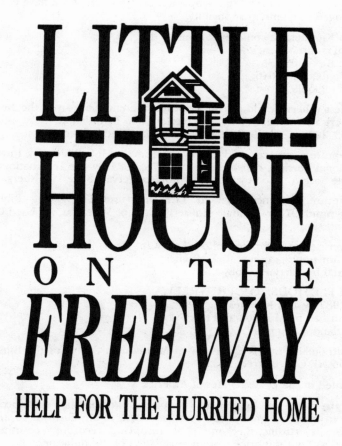

LITTLE HOUSE ON THE FREEWAY

HELP FOR THE HURRIED HOME

TIM KIMMEL

MULTNOMAH · PRESS

Portland, Oregon 97266

Some of the names of the people appearing in this book have been changed to maintain anonymity.

Tim Kimmel is a conference speaker for:
Generation Ministries
P.O. Box 31031
Phoenix, AZ 85046
(602) 996-9922

Unless otherwise indicated, Scripture references are from the New American Standard Bible, © The Lockman Foundation 1960, 1962, 1963, 1968, 1971, 1972, 1973, 1975, 1977. Used by permission.

Scripture references marked NIV are from the Holy Bible: New International Version, copyright 1973, 1978, 1984 by the International Bible Society. Used by permission of Zondervan Bible Publishers.

Scripture references marked TLB are from The Living Bible, copyright 1971 by Tyndale House Publishers, Wheaton, Ill. Used by permission.

Cover design by Bruce DeRoos/Lois Kent Davis
Author photographer: Rick Mueller
Edited by Larry R. Libby

LITTLE HOUSE ON THE FREEWAY
© 1987 by Tim Kimmel
Published by Multnomah Press
Portland, Oregon 97266

Multnomah Press is a ministry of Multnomah School of the Bible, 8435 NE Glisan Street 97220

Printed in the United States of America

Library of Congress Cataloging-in-Publication Data

Kimmel, Tim.
    Little house on the freeway.

    Bibliography: p.
    1. Christian life—1960-   . 2. Marriage—
Religious aspects—Christianity. 3. Family—Religious life.
I. Title.
BV4501.K4933   1987   248.4   87-15395
ISBN 0-88070-205-2

    88 89 90 91 92 93 – 10 9 8 7 6 5 4 3

CONTENTS

To Darcy,

who brings more calm and confidence to

a home than this man deserves.

FOREWORD

MANY good books analyze the garden variety problems almost all of us face at some time in our marriages—poor communication, the need for financial planning, handling disagreements. But Tim Kimmel's book is the first I've seen that points us to one of the major underlying causes of fractured homes and unsatisfying marriages—our natural bent toward busyness.

In the short run, there's nothing wrong with being busy. All of us enjoy days filled with life and activity. But for many of us, our everyday schedules have become so crowded that activity has become a substitute for intimacy.

As I travel and speak around the country, I see the harried faces of hundreds of couples burdened with deepening lines of uncertainty and unrest. I often hear a husband or a wife say, "If we just had more time together" or "If we could only slow down the pace we're on. . . ." A week or even a single day of genuine rest comes into their lives about as frequently as an appearance of

Halley's Comet. What I found in the book *Little House on the Freeway* is an answer to the restless pace and hurried lifestyles that so characterize our out-of-breath society. Tim doesn't tell us to pack our bags and hike backwards in time to a more peaceful existence. All of us know that even those "out of the way" places often have a satellite dish in the backyard and imminent plans for an easy-access freeway. What Tim gives us is a practical way to deal with the real life pressures that rob us of rest and steal our joy.

I'll have to admit there are times when everyone in the Smalley family seems hurried and out of breath. If your family is like mine, and you've added more activities to your life but are enjoying it less, you'll find help and hope in these pages.

Genuine rest is on the endangered species list in many homes. Why not turn the page and discover, as I did, how God's rest can add life and zest to your family.

Gary Smalley
Phoenix, Arizona
May 1987

ACKNOWLEDGMENTS

I owe special thanks to . . .

Larry Libby and the staff at Multnomah Press . . .
you were a great fourth quarter team.

John Trent . . .
your guidance and confidence made the difference.

Kory Schuknecht, Barry Asmus, and Doug Childress . . .
your encouragement and advice were priceless.

The Board of Generation Ministries . . .
for keeping the platform strong.

Jean Harkey . . .
for your tireless assistance.

Jamie Drosse . . .
for your commitment to details.

The prayer Team and Caring Conquerers . . .
He heard you loud and clear!

Dave & Karen Cavan and Dennis & Mary Marketic . . .
this wouldn't have happened without you.

Karis, Cody, and Shiloh . . .
you've taught me more about rest than you'll ever know.
I'll be home for dinner.

CHAPTER 1

In Search Of Peace and Quiet

W HATEVER happened to uncluttered and un-complicated lives?

Maybe every generation asks the same question. But not every generation has had to deal with pressures like ours has. We're teetering on the edge of the twenty-first century knowing that we must plunge into the future but not sure we're ready.

It seems like only yesterday we were plowing the lower forty, walking to school, going to town once a week, and getting to bed by eight o'clock. Millions of people who made their debut on our planet in the early part of this century remember when their town looked like the set of "Little House on the Prairie."

But Walnut Grove has changed a lot since they added the Pizza Hut, the Seven-Eleven, and the unisex hair salon. Quiet, simple lives have given way to offramps, automatic teller machines, and Quarter-Pounders with Cheese.

Pa Ingalls wouldn't believe his eyes.

Life will never again be like it was when we lived in our quiet little houses on the prairie. We all live too close to the freeway to back away from its reality. Together we enjoy all of the benefits and conveniences of modern living. And together we suffer the inevitable consequences.

Moving from a muscle society to a mental society caught the family off guard. Revolutions in information, transportation, and mechanization have cost us dearly. Our sense of permanence, unity, and peace are being jeopardized by our hurried lifestyles. The family that makes it through life without bearing the marks of a hurried home is the exception, not the rule.

It's like the "Peanuts" cartoon that appeared in a Sunday morning paper. Lucy is offering one of her unsolicited observations about life to Charlie Brown.

"Life," she muses, "is like a deck chair. Some place it so they can see where they are going. Some place it so they can see where they have been. And some place it so they can see where they are at present."

Charlie Brown replies, "I can't even get mine unfolded!"

Many of us feel as if we can't get our lives unfolded! With all the worry and hurry around us, it's difficult to gain any kind of honest perspective. Sometimes it takes a whack on the side of the head just to get our attention.

THE HURRIED LIFESTYLE: UP CLOSE AND PERSONAL

Marshall's story:

Marshall sat in his car outside the cardiologist's office, his forehead against his hands on top of the steering wheel. Tears filled his eyes and fell into his lap.

The doctor's voice had been grim. He wasn't bluffing this time. "It's up to you, Marshall. Either slow down *immediately*, or put your affairs in order and say your goodbyes. I know my cardiology, and I can guarantee that if you don't back off the pace you're on, you won't live to see another Christmas. We've talked about this before, and I don't know how to warn you any stronger. It's got to stop, NOW!"

Marshall's hands gripped the wheel. *How could it be?* He had it all. He was a Christian—a leader in his church. He had a loving, devoted wife and three fairly normal kids. Life had even dished him out a generous piece of the American pie.

An overwhelming feeling of betrayal swept over him, bringing anger after the tears.

For Marshall, the words "slow down" were a terrible blow. And even with the doctor's warning ringing in his ears, cutting his schedule seemed flat wrong. Slow down? It was out of the question—even if he *wanted* to. His commitments and creditors would not allow him the luxury. He was hooked, frustrated, and tired . . . so tired.

How had he ever climbed onto such an accelerating treadmill? Days filled with obligations. Nights filled with distractions. Meals choked down on the run. He knew he was bucking terrible odds by continuing his frantic pace, but . . . well, there was just so much to *do*.

Like many of us, Marshall was in desperate need of genuine rest—yet was unwilling to ask the hard questions and make the difficult decisions involved in finding it.

Marsha's story:

Marsha was a hurried woman. She was a hurried wife and a hurried mother. Her home was equipped with the latest appliances designed to do the mundane so she could be freed up to do the EXCITING. Perhaps "exhausting" would be a better word.

Marsha was the only woman on her block with the "luxury" of staying home and raising her children. This meant that she had even more time than a working mother to jam in daily obligations to her church, children, in-laws, community, country club, babysitting co-op, and former sorority.

Balancing the school and special events schedule of one pre-teen and two teenagers, and driving a taxi service to school, soccer practice, band rehearsal, and swim lessons was only the tip of the iceberg. Add in aerobics, two women's Bible studies, volunteering at the hospital, the ever-present demands of cleaning a large house, and the need to be "fresh and at her best" when her executive husband came home from work, and Martha was t-i-r-e-d. Physically, emotionally, and spiritually, Martha was in deep need of genuine rest.

Perhaps as an effort to recapture this missing element in her world, Marsha took a daily, one-hour vacation. At 2:00 P.M. every weekday she would retire to her room, get comfortable on her bed, pick up the remote control, push the appropriate button and make channel forty-two appear. Then, for the next fifty-eight minutes, Martha would join Laura Ingalls and her family as they experienced life in their "Little House on the Prairie."

In her break from a disorienting, fast-paced schedule, Marsha envied the Ingalls' uncomplicated lifestyle. Choices were fewer—and seemingly easier to make. The list of necessities for happiness was still food, clothing, and shelter.

When did it all change? Marsha wondered as the Little House theme signaled the end of yet another episode. *When did the list of necessities for happiness get so long? Somewhere between yesterday and tomorrow it's been expanded to include skateboards, contact lenses, curling irons, VCRs, microwave ovens, compact disc players and purple hair mousse. How did life get so complicated?*

Marsha's life was "full" to the point of overflowing, but on "empty" when it came to inner contentment. Her spirit craved rest the way an exhausted body craves sleep. Yet she had no idea where to find it.

REST IS (NOT) OUT OF THE QUESTION

Marshall and Marsha are not alone, and they are not without hope. In the midst of the most hurried and haggard schedule they can discover, and so can we, lasting calm that reaches into the very center of our lives.

God wants us to enjoy genuine rest. Not just the "good night's sleep" kind of rest that satisfies the body, but an internal rest that bathes the soul in contentment.

It's a relief to know that rest is not out of the question. There are elements of rest which can be appropriated into our lives. In the pages that follow we will look at the foundation for genuine rest and six crucial battlegrounds where the struggle for rest must be waged.

But there is a paradox ahead. As we will see in later chapters, these very elements that bring us rest may also move us to the outer limits of our "comfort zones."

WHEN A PARADOX BECOMES A PRINCIPLE

I'm certain this sense of paradox wasn't lost on Joshua as he stood poised to cross the Jordan River. Forty years of restless wandering were behind him. He and Caleb were the only survivors of the original gathering of adults to leave Egypt four decades before. The decaying remains of the bickering and idolatrous generation who had left with them lay lifeless under the Sinai sands.

Moses, his leader and close friend, was the last to go. Now General Joshua, a fearless spy and decorated warrior, was commander of Israel.

Behind him stood the offspring of the "wilderness" group, women and children anxious to stop wandering. Beside him stood thousands of armor-clad untried soldiers anxious to get their first taste of battle. Before him sprawled the unconquered mountains and valleys of the promised land.

The assurance of God's own words washed across his spirit as he prepared his people to claim their promised real estate.

The LORD your God is giving you rest and has granted you this land (Joshua 1:13 NIV).

Ahead of Joshua lay struggle and hardship, behind him only death in the desert. Yet all was not lost. God had spoken a promise that must have brought incredible hope to the anxious commander's heart. God had told him that as surely as he would enter the land, he would enter into "rest" as well.

The paradox is really a principle for us today. *Genuine rest is never far away from the middle of a challenge.* Joshua's giants might have been Canaanite warriors, but the giants facing you and me cast intimidating shadows as well. As we will see in detail, the secrets of genuine rest promised to the nation of Israel are still keys to living life to the fullest today.

Years ago a contest was held in which artists were invited to paint a picture of peace. The entries were eventually narrowed down to just two. The first artist had interpreted perfect peace by painting a quiet lake cradled high in the lonely mountains. The second artist painted a thundering waterfall . . . with the branch of a birch tree bending over the foam. On the fork of that limb, wet with spray, a robin sat undisturbed on her nest.

Many of us would love to be able to identify with that robin. Our lifestyles are filled with unavoidable stress and activity that doesn't look like it's going to go away. In learning what God's Word has to say about genuine rest, we too can gain an unshakable calm. Even in the middle of the storm.

CHAPTER 2

Seven Marks of a Hurried Family

Do you know a hurried family? ("Do I know a hurried family? Why do you think I'm reading this book?") If you are trying to keep pace with other high-gear families in these closing years of the twentieth century, being hurried is hard to avoid.

Over the past fifteen years I've watched the speed at which we live our lives go from second gear to *overdrive*. In counseling individuals and couples across the country, I've observed at least seven characteristics that mark hurried families. Separately they're bad. Combine them and they're deadly. They attack the faith, joy, and love needed for a family to be at rest.

I'd like you to join me for a stroll down a typical street in a typical American neighborhood. The houses are cloned by architects, the families by a hurried society. We'll stop by seven homes for a closer look. As we peer through the windows, don't be too surprised if you catch a glimpse of your *own* family.

THE BAILEYS: CAN'T RELAX

Meet the Baileys . . . if you can. It's hard to get to know them because their schedule doesn't allow much time to cultivate close friends. But they do have a lot of acquaintances. They meet them through the numerous "projects" that make up their day.

Frank, a salesman, sets the pace. He's so used to a crowded schedule that he feels guilty when he isn't "in motion." He belongs to two civic clubs, oversees the United Fund Drive every year, coaches soccer, plays racquetball twice a week, trains for an annual marathon, teaches junior high Sunday school, and maintains a beautifully landscaped yard. His latest toy is a cellular carphone.

His wife, Leslie, works part-time. That way, she has plenty of time left over to be busy. Leslie is always creating new projects. It's interesting to visit their house once a year to see all the changes she has made. "Redecorating is the way I relax," she's always saying.

Like her husband, Leslie is committed to physical fitness and civic improvements. She works out every day and volunteers several hours a week to her political party. The only time her neighbors get to visit with her is when she knocks on their door with yet another petition.

The Bailey kids are busy being president of this and captain of that. They seldom have time to get into trouble. Most parents would love to have them as their children.

The Baileys are the envy of the neighborhood. On the surface they look ideal, but their industrious veneer hides one of the standard marks of a hurried family. *They can't relax.*

It's not that they *don't* relax, it's that they *can't* relax. What some would describe as resourceful is just a cover-up for restlessness. It's their way of not having to be idle. Charles Swindoll capsulizes their dilemma:

Busyness rapes relationships. It substitutes shallow
frenzy for deep friendship. It promises satisfying
dreams, but delivers hollow nightmares. It feeds the
ego, but starves the inner man. It fills the calendar,
but fractures the family. It cultivates a program, but
plows under priorities.[1]

The Baileys aren't bad, they're just too busy.

THE GRAHAMS: CAN'T ENJOY QUIET

You know when you are nearing the Graham's residence by the sounds blaring from behind their walls. It's
hard to tell exactly what the music is, however, because
of the different strains emanating from different rooms.
You might say the place is filled with entertainment.

As you walk in the front door you notice the television talking to itself in the family room. "Elevator music"
slurps out of the intercom, "top forty" grinds from their
thirteen-year-old's room, and "heavy metal" rock screams
from their sixteen-year-old's bedroom (it's the farthest
from the parents'). Janet Graham is talking on the phone,
permanently fixed under her chin, while stirring a cake
mix for tonight's dinner. From her kitchen vantage point,
she keeps an eye on the TV blaring in the dining room.
Her favorite afternoon talkshow host has just begun in-
terviewing a nutritionist who promises the diet to end
cellulite forever.

Gordon Graham loves "Big Band" jazz. You can usually hear Count Basie before you can see Gordon's car.
He likes to eat as soon as he arrives home. Tonight will
be no exception. The family will gather in the dining
room for supper. As usual, they will find out more about
the cast of M*A*S*H's day than their own.

Every Graham sleeps with his or her radio on. Their
bodies slumber, but their spirits do not rest. They are a

sad example of the second mark of a hurried family; *they can't enjoy quiet.*

The Grahams are intimidated by silence. As their hearts cry out for rest, they answer back with entertainment. By keeping their brains occupied with external sounds, they don't have to face the emptiness within. Noise is the Valium that helps them cope with inner restlessness.

The greatest gift the Graham family could receive would be for lightning to strike a local substation and shut off the power for several days. But knowing Gordon Graham, he'd just crank up the Honda generator he keeps for just such "emergencies." He bought it last summer for their two-week camping trip. They almost couldn't get it in their van because the video cassette recorder and television took up so much room.

THE JONESES: NEVER FEEL SATISFIED

As we walk toward the end of the block, the noise from the Graham's house is only a faint din in the distance. Turning to the right, you can't help being impressed by the two-story Tudor style house about halfway down the street. It's the largest and most beautifully manicured home in the community. That's the Joneses. You know them, they're the ones everyone is trying to keep up with.

Brian Jones is a professional landscaper. Sharon Jones is a professional shopper. She also sells real estate. They both enjoy the same hobby—reading catalogs. Sharon's best friends are her two daughters, Molly and Mindy. They spend most of their time developing their friendship at the mall. They never come home empty-handed.

Michael, their youngest son, is preoccupied with upgrading. He is upgrading his bike, his computer, his skateboard, his image, and his friends. He's a chip off the old block.

Michael's father gets a new car as soon as they are showcased. He's had four boats in six years. He's the only guy I know who had an addition built onto his pool.

The Joneses telegraph the third mark of a hurried family. But contrary to what you might think, it is *not* materialism. With the economic blessings that the average American family enjoys, most homes would be considered materialistic. The Jones family is badgered by a far more serious and subtle enemy. *The Joneses are never satisfied.* They aren't satisfied with what they have, where they are, or what they are.

For this family, contentment is always just around the corner—in the latest shipment from L.L. Bean, in being the first one on their block to have one. One *what?* It doesn't really matter, as long as they're first. They are a family robbed of rest. They have failed to see that satisfaction is a choice.

THE GARDNERS: AN ABSENCE OF ABSOLUTES

The somewhat predictable Joneses are a contrast to their neighbors, Steve and Millie Gardner. The only thing you can be certain of with the Gardners is their uncertainty. They display an overwhelming lack of permanence in their family—and have a hard time imagining life beyond the moment.

Their home is a collection of unfinished projects, cluttered with unneeded items bought on impulse and in bad need of repair. They are great at starting but poor at finishing . . . at pursuing ideas without a plan . . . at searching but never finding . . . at consistently confusing yes and no.

They've tried several churches. The Presbyterians were too formal. The Baptists were too narrow. The Charismatics were too casual. They enjoyed the fellowship and they needed the leadership, but their vacillating standards denied them a safe harbor in church. It wouldn't be long before someone would get close enough to them to see their inconsistencies. Running was their only tolerable option.

Both Steve and Millie have had occasional lapses in fidelity. Steve rationalized it as passing indulgences. Millie was just adding a little flavor to her routine existence. Each marital glitch left them further apart.

Steve is being scrutinized by the IRS. They're sure that he keeps two sets of books. In time, he, like all men with his problem, will get caught. People with shifting standards fail to see that the Piper always gets paid.

Steve and Millie are a good example of the folly of situational ethics. They make up the rules as they go along. As far as they are concerned, Moses received the "Ten Suggestions" on Sinai, not the Ten Commandments. It's all backfired on them, though, and their children are the unfortunate victims.

Take Jeremy, for instance. He's trying to graduate from high school. It's become a real challenge, since he is a habitual cheater. He lacks basic skills, and therefore lacks confidence. He copes by regularly getting high. His parents don't like it. But neither they nor he feel they are qualified to criticize him.

His sixteen-year-old sister is an even sadder commentary on the vacillating Gardners. She developed early. Her father encouraged her to dress in a way that accented her figure. If he knew that his favorite poker buddy had molested her when she was twelve, he'd kill him. She's got big problems now. Two months ago she got pregnant. Her parents are demanding that she abort the baby, but she wants to keep it and rear it herself.

It hurts to watch the restless, wandering Gardners. They refuse to recognize an absolute authority in their lives and therefore never feel sure of themselves. They go to church and occasionally read the Bible, but they are not convicted by it enough to let it guide them in specific decisions. They are restless because they live for the immediate at the expense of the permanent.

Every neighborhood has a few Gardners living in it. You watch them take one insecure step after another through a daily maze and shake your head. I pity the Gardners. It's as if they're lost on the sea of life, always pursued by a nagging sense of guilt. They need rest.

THE MOORES: SUFFERING SERVANTS

As we leave the Gardners arguing in the background, we come to a house that is always engulfed in activity. That's the Moore's.

The Moores live in every neighborhood. They are always there when you need them, quick to sympathize, ready to sacrifice.

When the church lost its Boy Scout leader, Sydney Moore came to the rescue. When a family from Sunday school class had their house gutted by fire, the Moores immediately took them in. If you need your car fixed, your house painted, your kids watched, you call the Moores. They have time to nurture everyone else's marriage and family life—except their own. Their marriage, their kids, and their spirits feel the neglect. Lately, their bodies have been showing the neglect. Sydney is quick to take time to meet you for breakfast to hear your problems but can never seem to find time to exercise.

They are great people who do wonderful things for others, but they are unhappy. Why? Because they do good things for wrong reasons. Their sympathetic gift is more often a cover-up for their own insecurities. They need approval. They need to hear the compliments in order to convince themselves that they are valuable.

We all love the Moores. At some time or another, we all *need* the Moores. But, we don't want to *be* the Moores. Their struggle for approval makes us tired. They are marked as a hurried family because they don't know how to handle their insecurities. They are denied rest by their inordinate need to be liked.

THE NEWBERRYS: A STORM BENEATH THE CALM

We wave to Grace Moore as she pulls out of her driveway to take dinner to a couple who just moved into the neighborhood. Directly across the street the Newberry's home is a welcome sight for our hurried eyes. Finally we've found a family who seem to have grasped the concept of rest.

As you get to know the Newberrys, you are impressed by the calm, controlled way they move through life. Most of what they do, they do with relative ease. It's reflected in the peace they exude.

Norma, in particular, comes across well to her friends. She never seems to be in a rush. Her car is usually five miles under the speed limit. The best way to describe the way that she has decorated her house is "peaceful."

Beneath Norma's calm smile, however, hides her little secret. Her smile masks a plaguing problem that she successfully shrouds from her family and friends.

Norma Newberry is a confirmed, card-carrying *worrier*. Different from the legitimate worries that should accompany the question marks of life, she's shadowed by the irrational worry of a person who can't stand to encounter circumstances which she can't control. Sure, we all like to have as much control as possible over any given situation, but a healthy outlook on life realizes that life has its uncertainties. We are at the mercy of many variables.

That's not Norma's style. When she was a little girl her daddy walked out on her. Her mother did an excellent job of raising her, but the devastation to her security system left her unsure of herself. She compensated on the outside but never gained confidence on the inside.

Her childhood trauma has haunted her throughout her life. It boils down to two gnawing frustrations: *fear of loss and desire for gain*.

Daily she worries that Ken will lose his job. Who cares that he has been secure in his position for over eighteen years? She is certain that one day he's going to come home carrying a cardboard box filled with the personal belongings from his office.

She worries that her children are going to be in an accident. If they are late coming home from school or an appointment, she calls the police and local hospital to check the accident report. When her son went to camp for the first time, she invented lame reasons for calling him every day to make sure he wasn't upset or injured. She worries that her mother (who has great health for her age) is going to have a heart attack. She guards her close friends and hates it when they develop new relationships, fearing that competitive relationships might turn them against her. Her worry never shows on the outside. It would be better if it did. It's just beneath the surface; the storm beneath the calm.

Rest eludes the Newberry house because one member courts fear. They are not a weak family—just *fragile*. Worry is a series of hairline fractures running through the foundation of their home. If everything goes well, they will adequately endure, but that is one "if" they can't count on.

Their home is one you are anxious to enter but can't wait to leave. Fear has such a throathold on one person living in it that everyone feels edgy. It's a shame. The Newberrys are such nice people.

THE EVANSES: "WORLD CLASS" OVER-ACHIEVERS

We'll drop in on one more home on Hurried Street: the residence of Allen and Minya Evans. An all-American family, they fail to enjoy rest because they are overachievers. They are the by-product of a competitive society that only applauds winners.

Allen Evans's love affair with winning started as a child. His father didn't have much time for him. He even hinted that Allen lacked the raw talent needed to be great. Allen countered by excelling in school, Little League, and school government. He was pleased to see his father's unabashed approval. Once he realized what it took to be accepted, he honed his talents and skills. He would be a "textbook" winner.

National Honor Society, Ivy League school, Fortune 500 company, and taking the ladder of success three rungs at a time became his mark. He's still proving to his father that he not only has the raw talent to be great but that he *is* great. Not that his father cares about it either way. The elder Mr. Evans died when Allen was still in high school. But there's not a day in Allen's life when he doesn't sense his father's ghost frowning over his shoulder.

His wife, Minya, is the daughter of immigrants. She was born after her parents had already established themselves in America. They were blessed by the land of opportunity but never forgot what it was like to live where there was little hope. They pushed their daughter to be the best. Their motives were pure. They meant it for good, but they inadvertently robbed her of rest. They did it by not teaching her how to accept defeats. She married a male clone of herself, and they've been winning ever since . . . well, almost.

Allen and Minya don't flaunt their wealth, but they know that their marriage would be in peril if they lost it. The reason they know this is because they nearly lost their fortune—and their relationship—about four years ago.

Allen made what most stockbrokers would consider a shrewd purchase of a new and promising stock. As happens occasionally, it turned out to be a lemon. He had transferred the money to his broker without consulting Minya. When things went bad and there was no other choice, he informed his wife. That's when World War III broke out in their home.

To be fair to Minya, it was a substantial loss. But for both of them, it was an unbearable lesson in reality. Unfortunately, they didn't do very well on their lesson. For a long period of time, Minya's confidence in Allen was shattered. Even more surprising was the depression that overwhelmed Allen. He couldn't believe that he could lose so much. He couldn't believe that he could come so close to losing it all.

Their son has a mildly deformed foot that held him back from making the first string on his soccer team. After three games of watching his son sit on the bench, Allen had had enough. He pulled his son off the team. The coach begged him to reconsider, but the pleas fell on deaf ears.

The Evanses aren't able to rest because they don't know how to lose. They are happy *only* when they are succeeding. Because success is always temporary, they push themselves and their children from one victory to the next. Their laurel leaves wither on their restless heads. They are a family with much pride but little joy. Their home suffers because they have failed to appropriate the keys to genuine rest.

A VISIT TO YOUR HOME

We leave behind seven restless families. Their houses might be on the best streets in their community, but the families are stuck on a spiritual and emotional dead end. With the tour over, I wonder what we would see if we peeked in on your family? Maybe we would see traces of the problems frustrating our seven not-so-imaginary friends.

Let's get personal. Have you seen yourself in any of these families we visited? I suppose it would be hard *not* to. Traits from families like yours and mine contribute to the collage we've called "Hurried Street." Let's review the seven tell-tale marks of a hurried home and then practice some honest evaluation.

My home may be hurried if . . .

we're so busy that we can't relax
we're uncomfortable with quiet
we're seldom satisfied with what we have
we live our lives with shifting situational
   standards
we are over-worked and under-appreciated
we worry about things we can't control
we aren't happy unless we're successful

Like you, I'm concerned about the accelerating pace our society sets up. I want to give my family the gift of rest—to be able to move off Hurried Street forever. Unless I miss my guess, you'd probably like to do the same. How do we turn the tables in our favor? It starts with some tough but honest self-evaluation.

To help us get started, let's take an unhurried look at three common threads that run through hurried households.

The First Thread: An Inability to Believe

Our culture questions the power of God at the same time it emphasizes the adequacy of man. We are encouraged to reject the God who is there in order to become the gods that we're not. Those of us committed to a personal God, a God actively involved in our lives, find ourselves in conflict with an environment that makes it too easy to doubt.

The Second Thread: A General Discontent

Being hurried and restless throws a wet blanket over our joy. It reminds me of a mild fever. You're not sick enough to stop what you are doing and go to bed, but it's impossible to enjoy much of what you *are* doing.

The constant push of contemporary life does that to us. Eventually, the confusion leads us to make wrong conclusions about what real joy in life is. Like a nagging stone in our shoe, restlessness makes it hard to enjoy the scenery as we make our seventy-year hike through time.

The Third Thread: A Lack of Genuine Intimacy

Intimacy is the strength that runs through each link of the family chain. With it, a family can endure anything. Without it, we are at the mercy of our hurried lifestyles. Intimacy provides the immune system for the soul. It battles the psychological infections of discouragement, rejection, inadequacy, insignificance, and insecurity. Being assured of acceptance gives us confidence. Confidence gives us the ability to endure. Rushed schedules rob us of time needed to develop personal relationships. Too many people are duped into thinking that a little bit of "quality" time compensates for the lack of "quantity" time. As we learn what it means to be at rest in the Scriptures, we'll discover several keys to developing communication and intimacy that are missing in hurried homes.

Each of these common threads of unrest place family relationships in a straitjacket. Why, then, is it so easy to fall victim to a hurried home? What sets us off on a highspeed cross-country race without a road map?

THE LURE OF A HURRIED HOME

It's funny how easily we can find ourselves in a fast-forward mindset. It doesn't require a conscious effort. Actually, it is the logical outcome of the forces surrounding us each day.

I see it in my own family. The Kimmels have found that being hurried comes naturally—while being at rest requires an ongoing appraisal of priorities. All of us who are serious about our spiritual life and our family life must counter the forces threatening our ability to maintain rest. What are these forces? They are the same ones frustrating the parents and teenagers who come to my office for help. They are the ones that may be taking their toll on your family too.

A Hurried Home: Our Culture Values It

The first pressure comes from a society that *values being hurried*. We have grown accustomed to having everything NOW. We are the instant generation. We like to tell a sign behind a restaurant what we'd like for dinner and then expect the people inside to have it prepared by the time we pull our car around to the serving window. We cut projects down to the wire because we know we can ship a package anywhere in the continental U.S. (and now abroad) within twenty-four hours. Automatic teller machines give us instant cash. Microwave ovens give us immediate meals. Modern malls give us sudden debt.

We have a love affair with haste. We call it convenience, and there is no doubt that many of our modern conveniences have made some of the mundane duties of life more tolerable. But there is a subtle programming that goes on at the same time. It's not long before we drive our lives the way we drive our cars—too fast.

I was reading in the paper the other day about a local entrepreneur. He wanted to make getting a video movie more convenient, so he introduced home delivery with next day pickup. You simply call and order your movie from the monthly list they send you, and within a few minutes it will be delivered to your door. Now if we can get this man to open up a pizza delivery business in conjunction with his video service, we could save ourselves the hassle of having to answer the front door twice!

There is nothing wrong with convenience. It's just that sometimes it frees us up to complicate our lives in a dozen new ways. Every year our consumer oriented culture invents hundreds of convenience devices which make it inconvenient and difficult to relax.

A Hurried Home: Business Rewards It

If culture values being hurried, it's because *business rewards it*. The second pressure demanding a hurried lifestyle is not one we can easily alter. The business community too often holds the family hostage. Winning in the business arena requires that we stay ahead of the competition. Marriage and family commitments must accommodate the whims of the company president obsessed with outperforming his peers. Many times workers would like very much to rearrange their priorities, but don't dare say anything. They know they are too expendable to complain.

A major financial magazine recently published interviews with the "100 most successful executives" in the country. Listen to a comment from a man who has made the "top 10."

> Reaching the level of business success that I have requires total commitment. If your family is too demanding, *get a new family*. That's what I did. . . .

While I applaud this man's honesty, he deserves anything but praise for the way he left his family in the dust. He's not alone. It seems that each rung of the corporate ladder has its own set of new demands. Frequently, a raise in salary represents a raise in anxiety. More money for more things and less time to enjoy them. If society is rough, business is often vicious.

A Hurried Home: The Media Exploits It

Business and society can't compete with the third pressure that deprives the contemporary family of rest: the pressure from the media. Relentless in its pursuit of the American family, it is the cultural architect of the hurried lifestyle. Its very existence depends on keeping us restless.

Paperback romance novels take their readers to exotic places and make changing marital partners as casual an endeavor as changing clothes.

Soap operas teach us that the essence of life is being rich, beautiful, and unsatisfied.

Saturday morning cartoons create a toy or doll and then build a program around it. Then they proceed to make our children feel inadequate if they don't have one of their very own.

Evening news teams deluge the American family with a journalistic format that tells *what*, but seldom *why*, and makes it a professional practice to never offer solutions. ("Here you are folks, more ammunition for your despair.") And if it isn't the books, magazines, or television shows themselves, hundreds of all too eager advertisers make the good life too attractive to pass up—even if a family has to experience terminal debt to achieve it.

Television presents family problems in an unrealistic light. No matter how complicated the problem, we know that it will be solved in one hour with two or three breaks to sell a chunk of the good life. Television families come up with clever lines and rosy prescriptions to even the most difficult problems they face. Watching them end each show with bushels of hugs and laughter programs us to think that problem solving is easier than it really is.

The media exploits the family . . . and loves every hurried minute it has to create discontent.

The Hurried Home: Our Egos Demand It

The truth is that I don't need society, a job, or even the media to create a hurried home. I can do a great job of it on my own. Man's fleshly ego *hungers* for an overloaded life. We become addicted to regular surges of adrenaline.

Our hurried lifestyle is a result of taking shortcuts in life. *Since the fall of man in the Garden of Eden, sin has refused to let us rest.* Stripped to its core, sin is "the desire to have it now." Sin is the enemy of time. It takes time to be organized. It takes time to meaningfully communicate. It takes time to develop intimate friendships. It takes time to build character in a child.

Warped by sin, our egos look for cheap shortcuts. Instead, we end up restless and dissatisfied with life.

Yet God offers hope. The exciting truth for the modern family is that genuine rest can be enjoyed today. It's a gift to the contemporary home in desperate need of a break from the rat race.

For those of you who are feeling dismayed, take heart. I was dismayed until I realized that God has provided a strategy for countering the pressures of life in the express lane. In our next chapter, we will lay the irreplaceable foundation for that strategy.

CHAPTER 3

The Foundation for Genuine Rest

CALAMITY has a sick sense of timing.

It doesn't believe in warnings, just surprises. It's not a stranger knocking at our front door, but a burglar coming in through a window. Though I've been spared many visits by calamity, the few I've had have grabbed me by my spirit and shaken their instruction into the deepest recesses of my heart. What I learned one cold December night in a sterile hospital room, you may learn in a different setting. But the lessons have a universal application for any soul yearning for genuine rest.

While my wife, Darcy, was in the hospital recovering from the Caesarean delivery of our third child, our other two children were left to my care. They didn't mask their anxiety as they watched their father trying to be mother. Frankly, their anxiety had merit.

I've never really struggled being a provider for my family. But when I not only have to bring home the bacon, but cook it too, there is cause for concern. My children know the extent of my skills in the kitchen. I can prepare a bowl of cereal, and I make a great tray of ice. I know the number for Domino's Pizza and the quickest route to the Golden Arches. Beyond that, I come up lame at meal time. Darcy was going to be in the hospital for five days. In my mind that calculated out to at least fifteen variations of cereal and ice . . . or a lot of Big Macs.

On the third night of my role as "Mr. Mom," I thought things were going pretty well. My kids had brushed a little harder to remove their cheeseburger and french fry breath, and we had shared bedtime prayers and a few choruses of "Jesus Loves Me" before both of my charges drifted into dreamland.

I crawled into my own bed and did a quick inventory of the day. As far as I was concerned, it couldn't have been improved. I had a great time with my two oldest children, enjoyed an excellent visit with my wife and new daughter, got some work done at my office, cleaned the house, and even paid a few bills. It was satisfying to sink into a deep sleep knowing that everything was "under control."

My style of sleeping resembles a mild coma. I make such a commitment to the process of slumber that it takes a lot to shake me awake.

Somewhere a phone was ringing.

I incorporated it into my dreams for a suspended moment until its persistence drew me up from the depths. My clock radio said it was only 11:30 P.M., but I felt as if I'd been asleep for hours.

I groped for the phone. It was Darcy. She was crying.

Having been married to Darcy for a decade and a half, I've become fairly good at recognizing whether her tears are of joy, hurt, or fear. Her unrestrained sobbing over the phone told me something was seriously wrong. She was petrified.

She had just been informed that our three-day-old daughter had stopped breathing. The alert nurses had gotten her lungs going again, but to be on the safe side they had her on a monitor.

In the time it took Darcy to transfer this information, my perfect day was ruined.

When you hear that your child may have a physical malfunction, you immediately assume the worst. Maybe it's an unconscious defense mechanism. If we imagine the darkest scenario, we aren't surprised when it happens—and are overjoyed when it doesn't.

At that moment, however, Darcy needed my assurance that everything was under control. The confidence that I spoke into the phone contradicted the worry that was knotting my insides. We prayed together, giving the whole situation to God. My voice was even and steady. I was a tower of spiritual strength . . . until I hung up the receiver. Then I reverted back to being human. My courage turned to jello. I was a man with words for others but none for myself. My heart began to literally ache inside my chest.

When a loved one is hurting or in danger, our first desire is to *do* something. To find yourself helpless in such a moment is one of the worst feelings imaginable. I was prepared to scale a wall, fight an army, run a marathon. But *wait?*

I knew the pain wasn't going to subside if I remained at home and did nothing. Besides, I suddenly wasn't very tired. I called my brother to stay with my sleeping kids, jumped into our station wagon, and sped off through the darkness to Scottsdale Memorial Hospital.

Hospitals take on their own personality at night. When I walked into the maternity wing the normal rush that accompanies labor and delivery had given way to calm. Nurses spoke in low, practiced tones. Music murmured faintly from a radio at the nurses' station. Everyone seemed to tiptoe. As I walked down the line of half-opened doors, I could see exhausted mothers trying to get one more decent night of sleep before they returned home to face several months of night shifts. I checked in with Darcy and then headed down the hall to the crisis nursery. The door whispered open.

Tiny Plexiglas beds held tightly wrapped little bodies—each representing the hopes and goals of moms and dads scattered across Phoenix. All of those little sleepers were important, but one bundle drew me to its side like a magnet. A small face with tightly shut eyes protruded from the end of a soft, pink flannel cocoon. The wires snaking out from underneath the covers ran to a cluster of machines monitoring vital signs.

The doctors briefed me, speculating what might be causing my baby's struggle to maintain normal breathing.

Then they left, and I sat down to watch, wait, and think.

Apnea. Well, there was a new word for my vocabulary. The dictionary defines it as "a transient cessation of respiration." But I didn't have the benefit of a dictionary definition that night. My introduction to the word came from the piercing alarm of a heart and lung monitor. *Apnea* defined itself a dozen times during the night, and each time brought the issue of life and death into glaring focus.

Most of us take the involuntary cadence of our heart and lungs for granted—until it becomes tentative. Watching the inconsistent dancing lines on the monitor made me realize what a tiny thread normal life hangs on.

I maintained my fatherly vigil for the next seven hours, alternating between watching the baby and praying, and rocking the baby and praying. Urgent predicaments are natural times for contemplation. It's amazing how much perspective you can gain on your crisis if you're given the luxury of being undisturbed for a few hours. I rocked back and forth in the silence, feeling the warmth of my baby girl's life through the blanket.

The night nurse attending the handful of infants in the nursery made me comfortable. She brought me a cup of coffee and we exchanged brief small talk. She commented that she had seen many fathers spend nights sitting next to their children. I told her that I realized my being there was not so much for my daughter's benefit as for mine. Love drove me to search for hope.

I might have been a trained seminarian and "Christian communicator" rocking in that chair, but somehow the comforting wisdom of practical theology seemed far from my thoughts. I was a typical father feeling the typical emotions that play in his heart when he watches his own flesh and blood struggling to win the first fight of her life.

INNER NEEDS

The crisis at my little daughter's side forced me to consider this matter of "rest" as I had never considered it before. Somehow I knew that if I was ever going to entertain the notion of genuine rest for my life—or for my daughter's—its certainty would depend on my ability to find rest *in that very situation*. On that very battlefield. On that very night.

It was a battle with two fronts: a restlessness on the *outside* created by circumstances beyond my control, and a restlessness on the *inside* created by my struggle with doubt and fear. I wanted to win on both fronts, but knew that victory over the battle inside me was the best way to insure victory over the battle against my circumstances.

As I wondered if my daughter would ever live to experience even a portion of the hopes and dreams that my wife and I had for her, it took me back to the grass roots issues of life. It wasn't important to me any more that she become a great pianist or master several languages. It was becoming clear that life boiled down to a handful of basic needs.

At the foundation of the concept of human rest are three inner needs. We build our lives on and around them. They are powerful needs that demand satisfaction, and are as essential to our survival as food, clothing, and shelter. If they are met in legitimate, healthy ways, our lives can experience a sweet contentment. Deny yourself any or all of these needs, and you will put into place all of the necessary ingredients for a restless life.

I settled into the rocking chair and stared at the little life in my arms. She was so new. Yet given a chance, her life would become a complicated blend of emotions, impressions, and experiences. But just as the various hues of the rainbow are shades of three primary colors, the complexities that make up life are only variations of three inner needs. *Love*, *purpose*, and *hope* were what she needed in order to feel complete.

Those three needs that I wanted so much to satisfy in her life as she grew older were the same needs that I needed to have fulfilled in myself if I ever wished to enjoy genuine rest.

Acceptance: The Need for Love

There is probably no greater inner pain than the pain of loneliness. Our culture might have popularized the cult of self-worship, but it is an empty shrine. We can make macho speeches, or play self-sufficient games, but our independent attitude is a thin veneer at best. Deep within every living soul is a gnawing need to be accepted.

We are made so by design. God put a perfect man in a perfect environment . . . yet Adam was lonely. Fashioned to be incomplete by himself, his heart longed for companionship. And it was because of his longing that God made a woman for him to love. Eve completed a heart that was meant to be bonded with another.

It's probably no colossal revelation that people have an inner need for love. The carved initials in the trees lining the elementary school playgrounds testify that the need for loving commitment begins early. It's not enough to have friends, we have to have *best* friends, and the pain experienced when friendship covenants are broken is the worst pain of all.

"Love is a two-way street," croons the Country and Western singer, "but my baby's changing lanes." A healthy person never gets good at being jilted. The thousandth time you've been rejected hurts just as deeply as the first. So fundamental is man's need for love that there is actually a physical consequence when love is removed. Children can literally die when they are starved of affection. *Marasmus* is the clinical expression, but the layman's dictionary would define it as simply "lack of love."

As a father drawn to a child in need, I was keenly aware of my own inner need for love. I knew that my ability to experience rest had contingencies. I had to know that I was loved—and had to feel a freedom in loving back. It was also obvious to me that love was one pledge I had to make to my daughter. Her physical problems could have been minor or serious, but they would seem insignificant to her if she had to go through life feeling unloved. The inner need for love was one area of her life in which I couldn't afford to fail.

Affirmation: The Need for Purpose

Love is a driving need that gives security, but we need purpose to feel significant. We need that little spark of attention from someone who believes in us. The mileage that the human spirit can derive from an affirming word is endless.

Most great achievers fall into two categories. They either have a purpose and are motivated to live it out, or they are madly driven to find one. Innate within the concept of rest is a confidence that you are significant.

A gifted classical musician comes to mind. Andor Foldes is now seventy-two, but he recalls how praise made all the difference for him early in his career. His first recollection of an affirming word was at age seven when his father kissed him and thanked him for helping in the garden. He remembers it over *six decades later*, as though it were yesterday.

But the account of another kiss that changed his life says a great deal about our inner need for purpose. At age sixteen, living in Budapest, Foldes was already a skilled pianist. But he was at his personal all-time low because of a conflict with his piano teacher. In the midst of that very troubled year, however, one of the most renowned pianists of the day came to the city to perform. Emil von Sauer was not only famous because of his abilities at the piano, but he could also claim the notoriety of being the last surviving pupil of Franz Liszt.

Sauer requested that young Foldes play for him. Foldes obliged the master with some of the most difficult works of Bach, Beethoven, and Schumann. When he finished, Sauer walked over to him and kissed him on the forehead.

"My son," he said, "when I was your age I became a student of Liszt. He kissed me on the forehead after my first lesson, saying, 'Take good care of this kiss—it comes from Beethoven, who gave it to me after hearing me play.' I have waited for years to pass on this sacred heritage, but now I feel you deserve it."[2]

Foldes no longer had a personal crisis. His kiss from Beethoven gave him a new sense of purpose.

When the internal well of confidence is dry, we all need a kiss from Affirmation. The problem that caused my brand new daughter to have difficulty breathing had drained my confidence. I wanted to rest in the reality of my significance—but it was difficult to see past my doubts.

Assurance: The Need for Hope

The trilogy of our inner needs is not complete without hope. Hope is the environment in which love and purpose breed contentment. It is the third strand that gives strength to our security and significance.

What good is it if you are making great time on a road to nowhere? Too many people are confused into thinking that a kind word and a sense of direction are enough. But hope is the glimmer of light on the horizon that says there is a reason to keep moving forward. The light might be faint and the road long, but the trip is bearable if we are certain there is a destination.

Hopes and dreams are often used as synonyms. In the Cinderella world that too many people live in, living happily ever after is followed by waking up to reality. Hope has to be more than that.

If dreams are made of sand, then hope is made of concrete. It's the bulkhead that withstands the pounding waves of life's stormy seas. It's the belief in the back of our minds that assures our spirits. But it must have a divine touch to last. Hope that is a product of human intuition is temporal. Those who allow God's love to cast its cross-shaped shadow over their human spirit give hope eternal life.

Love, purpose, and hope paid me a hospital visit. They weren't abstract concepts floating around in my brain. They were three friends wanting to settle down in my heart.

A LESSON FROM THE PAST

God has peculiar ways of bringing insights to our minds. With my daughter lying beside me and with my thoughts riveted on what life really means, two songs from two very different men came to mind. One played in my ears, and the other played in my heart. The songs conveyed the same message, but because of the men singing them, they stood in conspicuous contrast.

One man's story ended at a grave, the other's began there.

Up to that point, I hadn't been paying attention to the songs coming from the radio at the nurses' station. Most of the songs blended in with the background noises of the nursery. But my ears perked up when I heard the

sleepy DJ introduce one of the records he was about to
spin.

"Here's one for all of you who would like to be
asleep, but your troubles are keeping you awake."

He probably had to do some searching in the station
archives to find it, but once it started to play I had to
agree that its message was for me. The musical relic was
vintage Elvis Presley, but it had some advice for a confused father sitting beside his infant daughter in a quiet
Arizona hospital.

Elvis was singing his religious hit, "Crying in the
Chapel." It had been some time since I had heard the
song. I found myself drawn to its message in a new way.
The last verse of the song had the most encouragement
for me . . .

> You'll search, and you'll search
> But you'll never find
> A way on earth to gain peace of mind.
>
> Take your troubles to the chapel,
> Get down on your knees and pray.
> Then your burdens will be lighter,
> And you'll surely find a way.[3]

Inner peace is a gift that God wants to give us in
the middle of our crises. "Crying in the Chapel" was a
reminder that God is a sanctuary for restless, troubled
hearts.

But the song was contradicted by the singer.

I've always had a hard time disassociating a message
from its messenger. I couldn't help wondering how it was
that Elvis Presley could be so effective at singing advice
. . . and such a failure at taking it.

The Tomb of the "King"

When America was informed that the "King of
Rock 'n' Roll" was dead, millions of fans went into

mourning. For over two decades, Elvis Presley had embodied the soul of a young generation that wanted to shake, rattle, and roll. He was a living legend who lived too fast and died too soon.

When you look back over the life of a media phenomenon the size of Elvis Presley, it's hard to separate truth from fiction. Some fans were and still are so blindingly loyal that they don't want their memories altered by facts. But the circumstances surrounding his death give us a picture of the anguish that plagued him most of his life.

He went from rags to riches through the channels of the music industry. His controversial performances brought scorn from parents, accolades from teenagers, and money from both. Once his music became a mainstay, Elvis rode the popularity tidal wave with amazing skill.

He was generous. Never forgetting his humble beginnings, Elvis was quick to cheer on the underdogs and reward those who touched his life. When someone did him a favor he paid him back a thousand-fold.

He was religious. His musical eyeteeth were cut on the church hymnal. He knew there was a dimension of his life that needed and wanted God. Because we are a people who want to believe the best about our heroes, the public's view of Elvis's spiritual life is probably exaggerated. But we know that he acknowledged his need and desire for God at various times in his life.

He was personable. Those who knew him well saw him as an intensely fragile man. His circle of friends was small and his demands on them were great. With the responsibility of being his friend came the privilege of being loved back. The handful of people who got close to him testified to the seriousness he took in being a friend. He was loyal and sensitive.

But all was not well inside the heart of this star. Having everything that money could buy wasn't enough. Though surrounded by fans everywhere he went, he spent the prime years of his life overwhelmed by loneliness. Even with the handful of friends who stood close by him, his life never felt full. His life is a striking illustration that wealth and fame do not complete us. Elvis needed to love and be loved; he needed a sense of purpose and an assurance of hope.

He is proof that inner peace isn't for sale. As his popularity grew and the bottom line of his bank accounts stretched from seven digits to eight, his restlessness intensified. He could not find calm for his anxious spirit.

> You'll search, and you'll search,
> But you'll never find . . .

Elvis saw his enemy every time he looked in a mirror. He didn't need unforeseen calamities to bring him down. He did an adequate job of destroying himself without the help of circumstances. He had choices to make, but no adequate guide to use when making them. In the end, his choices cost him everything.

The only distinction between him and most other people overwhelmed by anxiety was that he was forced to live out his frustration with millions of people watching.

Elvis Presley died long before he needed to. Ravaged by drugs, the heart inside this media-made king gave out. When his unconscious body was found lying on the floor at Graceland, it marked the end of years of restlessness. He had all of what the world said should give us rest. But in the end, none of it could save him.

I rocked back and forth in my chair in the nursery. Elvis's song made me sad for him. I remember watching the news the day they buried him at Graceland. The line of mourners snaked out past his Memphis home for several city blocks. They were stunned that their king would leave them so soon. Years later, they still come, filing silently past his grave.

And then, as Elvis's song faded from the radio, I thought of another grave. A tiny plot in a simple cemetery on the edge of the Arizona desert.

There are no street signs directing you to the gravesite, nor crowds of mourners to mark its presence. The few times I've visited, I've had a hard time finding it. But to the west of the pond, and just a few feet from a lonely tree, the blades of bermuda grass are briefly interrupted allowing a modest, gentle statement carved in granite to peek through.

PUNKIN'
In loving memory
Jennifer Marie Strader
August 11, 1975—December 13, 1984

It's one of the few physical reminders that this little girl existed. But her brief life made an unforgettable impression on her family and friends, and the courage of her parents after her death gave me one of the best reasons why I'm sure that we can have rest no matter what.

"There Is Peace"

Resting my head against the back of the rocker, I closed my eyes and found myself humming a different song. The words and music were written by a special friend—Jennifer Strader's father, Rodger. When he wrote the song, he was a happily married young man with three children. He couldn't know that two years later he would only have two children to come home to at night.

Rodger Strader's song was prophetic, and in his loneliest moment, its message gave him rest.

Christian musicians may not have the fame and fortune of their counterparts in the secular music industry, but they have the same needs. When Rodger began his career as a Christian songwriter and singer, he wanted to love and be loved; he wanted to sense a purpose in his life and be stirred by the hope that he wrote and sang about. Next to his confidence in Christ, his family made the biggest contribution to those needs. His wife, Candy, came from a hymnwriter's family and understood the price that creative talent must pay to draw beautiful messages from its soul and put them to music. Rodger wrote beautiful songs and Candy raised beautiful children. Their daughter Jennifer was sandwiched between two handsome sons.

Singing about hope is a whole lot easier than believing in it, especially when one of your main reasons for living is suddenly and tragically removed from your life. Rodger's concept of hope was tested to its limit during the Christmas season of 1984.

It had seemed like such a "routine" day. Candy and her sister pulled up in front of the school that afternoon just as they did every weekday afternoon. The five kids they were collecting at the school came from the four corners of the campus. The last to get into the car was Jennifer.

She wasn't an extrovert, but she wasn't an introvert either. She had one of those mild dispositions that easily blended with everyone. Because she had the heart and soul of a peacemaker, friendships were made and maintained with ease. She was a pretty, quiet little girl contented with learning all the mysteries of childhood.

At a familiar corner, during a textbook left turn, tragedy paid a visit to the Strader family. A young man ran a red light and buried his truck into the side of the Straders' car. Jennifer's aorta was severed on impact, and her spirit immediately raced into the arms of the God she loved. There were injuries to the others that repaired with time, but for Roger and Candy, a hole was left in their hearts that time could not affect.

Neither of them said goodbye to their little girl.

Christmas season is a busy time for Christian musicians, especially if you've written popular Christmas musicals. Rodger was in Salem, Oregon rehearsing one of his musicals with a metropolitan church choir when he received the phone call that all parents dread.

Rodger instantly became an expert on the power of words. "There's been an accident, and Jennifer didn't make it." Nine common words taken from everyday language were put in an order that he had never heard nor wanted to hear in his life. When his brain interpreted them, his heart instantly broke. Words crushed his confident spirit with the force of a hammer. Rodger was surrounded by a stunned choir who shared a love for his Lord. But in spite of their circle of support, he felt completely alone.

Had he arrived at the airport a few minutes earlier, he would have caught the last plane to Phoenix. Instead, his uncertainty was compounded by the pain of waiting. His wife and boys had been injured, and he wouldn't feel confident about the extent of their injuries until he appraised them for himself. But one truth was a dark certainty . . . his little girl was lying in a Phoenix morgue, and nothing was going to change that fact.

A friend back in Phoenix hired a jet to fetch him from Portland. He sat in the back of the plane with only the noise of the engines and the endless night to keep him company. His mind jumped from worry about his wife and sons to memories of his Jennifer.

Stillness gives a spirit the ability to condense and compress a lifetime into a moment. The nine years of Jennifer Marie Strader danced across the screen within his mind. She had joined his walk through time when he was twenty-three and left when he was thirty-two, but the time that she shared the path with him made him a different man. A better man.

A little girl doesn't take up much space physically,

but her personality can stretch to every corner of a house. When Rodger retrieved his wife and sons and brought them home, it seemed that everywhere he looked he saw Jennifer. The artwork in her room and the projects that she left unfinished gave him an ache in his heart that made him want to groan out loud. He found himself wishing she would come walking into his study to ask for help with her homework.

Quiet can be an enemy to the broken heart, but it can also become an ally. The silence that stepped in where Jennifer stepped out was the silence in which Rodger Strader ultimately found rest. In the stillness of his study Rodger turned to the Inspiration of his songs . . . to the Author of his soul. He had prayed a hundred times in the twenty-four hours since his daughter's death, but the whirlwind of events surrounding the tragedy hadn't allowed him the luxury of inner rest. With the boys tucked in bed and his wife nursing her wounds along with her memories, Rodger retired to his study.

Rest is a visitor from heaven that wants to meet us in our tragedies. Unfortunately, there's something about our human pride that crowds this visitor out. Rodger was gifted with great emotional strength, and normally he could handle his problems. But this was too big for his defenses. Rodger found release. He wept. He poured out his pain before God.

God gave him rest—using familiar words and a familiar musical theme. Rodger crossed the room to his stereo, took out a tape, and cued his deck to a well-known song. The singer began the lines that Rodger had written two years before. He heard the song as if it were brand new. It was as though the song was not written by him as much as *for* him. The verses that he had written by watching other people's pain had a new meaning. He hung on to them as if he were hearing them for the first time.

In a world that's wracked by sin and sorrow,
There is peace.
When you find no hope for your tomorrow,
There is peace,
When it seems your heavy burden is much too much
to bear,
In Jesus, there is perfect peace.

There is peace, there is peace,
In the midst of every storm of life, there's peace;
If you'll put your trust in Jesus
And let Him have His way,
You'll find peace, perfect peace today.

If you're tired of all life's rush and hurry,
There is peace,
If your mind is filled with fear and worry,
There is peace,
When your problems overwhelm you and fill you
with despair,
In Jesus, there is perfect peace.

There is peace, there is peace,
In the midst of every storm of life there's peace;
If you'll put your life in Jesus
And let Him have His way,
You'll find peace, perfect peace today.[4]

Rodger was overwhelmed by a calm that came from above. Humbly, he accepted God's gift of rest for his tired soul. It was like a soothing salve from the hand of God.

My grace is sufficient for you, Rodger, because My power is perfected in your weakness.

A few days later, Rodger and Candy took their last look at the body that once was home to their daughter. They faced their darkest hour with a courage and dignity that only God could supply. They learned the foundational principle of rest that would carry them through the lonely years of adjustment that followed Jennifer's death. That principle is the realization that REST IS A CHOICE.

In many of our trials, there is no rest *from*, but there is rest *in*. Jesus said, "Come to me, all of you who are weary and overwhelmed by your circumstances, and I will give you rest. Take My yoke upon you and learn from Me, for I am gentle and humble at heart, and you shall find rest for your souls" (Matthew 11:28, my paraphrase).

The Lord's words are timeless. They stretch through twenty centuries to meet a couple standing by a child's simple grave or settle in the spirit of a confused father watching an infant take her first fragile breaths. They reassure us that our quest for rest is reachable. But it has to start *within* us before it can move *outside* of us. The pressures that create restless spirits can be countered by the elements of genuine rest. But these external solutions assume that we first have accepted God's internal solutions.

He loves us.

He made us with a purpose.

He guarantees us hope.

Rest is an attitude based on truth that we're certain of, regardless of the doubts. It's a deposit that our mind makes to the accounts of our hearts when we know the pressures aren't going to be quickly removed. We claim it more often and exercise it more regularly when we view it as a strategy for persevering, rather than an escape hatch.

We may learn it vicariously by watching cherished friends go through the nightmare of death, or we may learn it during an anxious night next to a struggling child. But its lessons *must* be learned.

God's rest doesn't guarantee that we will grieve or feel less anguish, but it does guarantee that we will hurt differently. It's a divinely altered perspective that won't let us lose sight of the fact that we are loved, even at the depth of our despair.

THE DAWN ALWAYS COMES

I was rocking my daughter when the hospital started to wake up. A fresh batch of coffee and a new batch of nurses signaled the end of night. I had endured my first all-night vigil with one of my children. Somehow I felt that I would have to have a few more of these before the last one left home. But I wasn't really fearful anymore. The alarms on the monitor had sounded several times that night, and with each one my heart rushed. Apnea signals had been counted, and slow heartbeats had been recorded on my daughter's chart. But as the dawn approached, I was calm.

My body hadn't left my child's side, but my heart had been to heaven. The two musicians who ministered to me had taught me a lot about what rest is, and what it isn't. I was confident about my daughter's condition. It wasn't some foolish mind game that says if I believe she'll be all right, then she will. Life's a vapor. There are no guarantees. My daughter's condition was treatable, and hopefully, she would outgrow it. But Jennifer Strader was proof enough to me that rest doesn't require a happy ending.

The rest that overwhelmed me came from a God who knew the pain of despair firsthand.

> He who did not spare his own Son, but gave him up for us all—how will he not also, along with him, graciously give us all things? (Romans 8:32 NIV).

A bloodstained cross and an empty tomb are the only guarantees. They make choosing rest easier.

I went by my wife's room to encourage her and then headed for home. On the way out I slipped into the nursery once more to plant a kiss on my little girl. The name scrawled on the card taped to her bed was a new one to me. My wife and I had decided on it a few days before she was born. Since her birth we had had second thoughts. But after the lessons she had taught me that night, I couldn't think of calling her anything else. Her name is from the Old Testament. It means "rest" and "tranquillity."

I bent down and kissed her on her tiny head.

"Thanks for the seminar on rest, *Shiloh*," I whispered. "Now wake up and start practicing your breathing."

CHAPTER 4

A Forgiving Spirit

I was thirty-four years old before I saw my first animated Disney movie. My daughter had accompanied me on a week-long speaking engagement, but bad weather made it hard for us to enjoy the outdoors. While exploring the local town we discovered that their only movie theater was showing Disney's *Jungle Book* during the matinée. We came in to see it on Tuesday and ended up coming back two more times.

One of the more memorable songs of the film was a toe-tapping tune by a fun-loving bear named Balou. This clumsy fellow danced around the jungle singing "The Bare Necessities," and it was hard to keep my daughter from getting up and dancing around the theater. For ol' Balou, happiness consisted of a few fundamentals: a banana, some good music, and a strong tree to scratch his back against.

Rest, in our stressful and demanding culture, is also found in a handful of fundamentals. It's not restricted to the experts in time management, or those fortunate enough to enjoy large chunks of discretionary time. It goes to those willing to continually maintain a few basic requirements.

As I study the Bible, I am impressed by the recurring themes that separate the rested heart from the restless. Those who have discovered rest seem to share at least six characteristics which set them apart. These characteristics are *non-negotiable principles*—essential if you want to enjoy a calm and rested spirit on an on-going basis.

THE FIRST NECESSITY:
WE MUST MAINTAIN
AN ATTITUDE OF FORGIVENESS

A person unwilling or unable to forgive can never be at rest.

As deeply as we may long for peace and rest, many of us find the corridors of our hearts haunted by ghosts from the past. Walking corpses. Grotesque, bitter spirits that moan and linger and rattle their chains . . . because we have refused to forgive people who have done us wrong.

How important is this? There are some men and women in an obscure little church outside of Seoul, Korea who could testify to the anguish that comes when we refuse to forgive.

Korea's chronicle stretches over hundreds of years. Bloody years. The careful student of that nation's history will notice that the Koreans have not been hostile toward their neighbors. For the most part, they have been a peace-loving nation. Yet they have found themselves consistently under attack by surrounding nations throughout their history.

Shortly after the turn of the century, Japan invaded, conquered, and occupied Korea. Of all of their oppressors, Japan was the most ruthless. They overwhelmed the Koreans with a brutality that would sicken the strongest of stomachs. Their crimes against women and children were inhuman. Many Koreans live today with the physical and emotional scars from the Japanese occupation.

One group singled out for concentrated oppression was the Christians. When the Japanese army overpowered Korea one of the first things they did was board up the evangelical churches and eject most foreign missionaries. It has always fascinated me how people fail to learn from history. Conquering nations have consistently felt that shutting up churches would shut down Christianity. It didn't work in Rome when the church was established, and it hasn't worked since. Yet somehow the Japanese thought they would have a different success record.

The conquerors started by refusing to allow churches to meet and jailing many of the key Christian spokesmen. The oppression intensified as the Japanese military increased its profile in the South Pacific. The "Land of the Rising Sun" spread its influence through a reign of savage brutality. Anguish filled the hearts of the oppressed—and kindled hatred deep in their souls.

One pastor persistently entreated his local Japanese police chief for permission to meet for services. His nagging was finally accommodated, and the police chief offered to unlock his church . . . for one meeting.

It didn't take long for word to travel. Committed Christians starving for an opportunity for unhindered worship quickly made their plans. Long before dawn on that promised Sunday, Korean families throughout a wide area made their way to the church. They passed the staring eyes of their Japanese captors, but nothing was going to steal their joy. As they closed the doors behind them they shut out the cares of oppression and shut in a burning spirit anxious to glorify their Lord.

The Korean church has always had a reputation as a singing church. Their voices of praise could not be concealed inside the little wooden frame sanctuary. Song after song rang through the open windows into the bright Sunday morning.

For a handful of peasants listening nearby, the last two songs this congregation sang seemed suspended in time.

It was during a stanza of "Nearer My God to Thee" that the Japanese police chief waiting outside gave the orders. The people toward the back of the church could hear them when they barricaded the doors, but no one realized that they had doused the church with kerosene until they smelled the smoke. The dried wooden skin of the small church quickly ignited. Fumes filled the structure as tongues of flame began to lick the baseboard on the interior walls.

There was an immediate rush for the windows. But momentary hope recoiled in horror as the men climbing out the windows came crashing back in—their bodies ripped by a hail of bullets.

The good pastor knew it was the end.

With a calm that comes from confidence, he led his congregation in a hymn whose words served as a fitting farewell to earth and a loving salutation to heaven. The first few words were all the prompting the terrified worshipers needed. With smoke burning their eyes, they instantly joined as one to sing their hope and leave their legacy.

Their song became a serenade to the horrified and helpless witnesses outside. Their words also tugged at the hearts of the cruel men who oversaw this flaming execution of the innocent.

> Alas! and did my Savior bleed?
> and did my Sovereign die?
> Would he devote that sacred head
> for such a worm as I?

Just before the roof collapsed they sang the last verse, their words an eternal testimony to their faith.

> But drops of grief can ne'er repay
> the debt of love I owe:
> Here, Lord, I give myself away
> 'Tis all that I can do!
> At the cross, at the cross
> Where I first saw the light,
> And the burden of my heart rolled away—
> It was there by faith I received my sight,
> And now I am happy all the day.[5]

The strains of music and wails of children were lost in a roar of flames. The elements that once formed bone and flesh mixed with the smoke and dissipated into the air. The bodies that once housed life fused with the charred rubble of a building that once housed a church. But the souls who left singing finished their chorus in the throne room of God.

Clearing the incinerated remains was the easy part. Erasing the hate would take decades. For some of the relatives of the victims, this carnage was too much. Evil had stooped to a new low, and there seemed to be no way to curb their bitter loathing of the Japanese.

In the decades that followed, that bitterness was passed on to a new generation. The Japanese, although conquered, remained a hated enemy. The monument the Koreans built at the location of the fire not only memorialized the people who died, but stood as a mute reminder of their pain.

Inner rest? How could rest coexist with a bitterness deep as marrow in the bones?

Suffering, of course, is a part of life. People hurt people. Almost all of us have experienced it at some time. Maybe you felt it when you came home to find that your spouse had abandoned you, or when your integrity was destroyed by a series of well-timed lies, or when your

company was bled dry by a partner. It kills you inside.
Bitterness clamps down on your soul like iron shackles.
    The Korean people who found it too hard to forgive
could not enjoy the "peace that passes all understanding."
Hatred choked their joy.
    It wasn't until 1971 that any hope came.
    A group of Japanese pastors traveling through
Korea came upon the memorial. When they read the
details of the tragedy and the names of the spiritual
brothers and sisters who perished, they were overcome
with shame. Their country had sinned, and even though
none of them were personally involved (some were not
even born at the time of the tragedy), they still felt a
national guilt that could not be excused.
    They returned to Japan committed to right a wrong.
There was an immediate outpouring of love from their
fellow believers. They raised ten million yen ($25,000).
The money was transferred through proper channels
and a beautiful white church building was erected on the
sight of the tragedy.
    When the dedication service for the new building
was held, a delegation from Japan joined the relatives
and special guests. Although their generosity was acknowledged and their attempts at making peace ap-
preciated, the memories were still there.
    Hatred preserves pain. It keeps the wounds open
and the hurts fresh. The Koreans' bitterness had festered
for decades. Christian brothers or not, these Japanese
were descendants of a ruthless enemy.
    The speeches were made, the details of the tragedy
recalled, and the names of the dead honored. It was time
to bring the service to a close. Someone in charge of the
agenda thought it would be appropriate to conclude with
the same two songs that were sung the day the church
was burned.
    The song leader began the words to "Nearer My
God to Thee."

But something remarkable happened as the voices mingled on the familiar melody. As the memories of the past mixed with the truth of the song, resistance started to melt. The inspiration that gave hope to a doomed collection of churchgoers in a past generation gave hope once more.

The song leader closed the service with the hymn "At the Cross."

The normally stoic Japanese could not contain themselves. The tears that began to fill their eyes during the song suddenly gushed from deep inside. They turned to their Korean spiritual relatives and begged them to forgive.

The guarded, calloused hearts of the Koreans were not quick to surrender. But the love of the Japanese believers— unintimidated by decades of hatred—tore at the Koreans' emotions.

> At the cross, at the cross
> Where I first saw the light,
> And the burden of my heart rolled away . . .

One Korean turned toward a Japanese brother. Then another. And then the floodgates holding back a wave of emotion let go. The Koreans met their new Japanese friends in the middle. They clung to each other and wept. Japanese tears of repentance and Korean tears of forgiveness intermingled to bathe the site of an old nightmare.

Heaven had sent the gift of reconciliation to a little white church in Korea.

Dealing with the Memories

The degree that you and I are open to experiencing inner rest is easily determined. It is equally proportionate to our willingness to forgive and to be forgiven. Some of you reading these words need not search any further to find out why you are not experiencing inner rest.

Unresolved conflict, cutting words, cruel rumors, and the isolation of your heart because of rejection siphon the joy away from even the most beautiful moments of life. The rest that you long for runs ahead of you—like a rainbow, forever out of reach. Maybe a few examples from people I have visited with will remind you of what I mean . . .

> You're taking a brief vacation from your shopping. You sit down in the coffee shop to enjoy some inner quiet when you hear a voice that spoils your appetite. The voice belongs to the boy who got your seventeen-year-old daughter pregnant. His next victim is hanging on his arm as he plops down at the other end of the counter. All you can remember is his reaction to the news that he was going to be a father. "Here's five bucks, why don't you get an abortion!" Your rage has bordered on homicide ever since.

> Your husband didn't say goodbye, he didn't leave a note, he just squeezed the trigger and it was over. You're not sure whom you hate the most, him for leaving you that way, or you for not being able to help him.

> He's a faithful grandfather. Never misses one of your son's soccer games. But you can't stand the sight of him there on the sidelines cheering your son, because when you were wearing a childhood uniform and racing down the sidelines, you could never hear his voice screaming you on to victory. You have time for your kid. Why didn't he have time for you?

> There they sit, as if nothing happened. Every Sunday they're frustratingly conspicuous in church. Her wardrobe is elaborate and expensive. They jump

into a fine car and go home to a fine house. But
their lifestyle was financed by many people in the
church who took out second mortgages or handed
over their life savings. The "opportunity" turned
out to be a scam, and the dream became a nightmare. Now he is safely guarded from repayment by
Chapter Seven of the bankruptcy code.

They borrowed your car. You were glad to help. Of
course they didn't mean to wreck it. It was obviously
an accident. But the insurance didn't cover all of
the repair. They felt that because your financial resources were greater than theirs, you could pay the
deductible yourself. You see her every now and then
driving around town. She waves from her brand
new car.

You get the point. We all have some hurt that loves
to come back and steal our joy. It sits in the back of our
memory waiting for an opportunity to be recalled. It's
always there, and no matter how hard we try, we can't
remove it. There are a myriad of advantages of being
human rather than a computer, but sometimes it would
be nice to have all of our painful memories stored on a
floppy disc stuck in the side of our head. A simple command could erase the hurt.

Even though we can't erase the hurts that lie stored
in the file drawers of our memory, we *can* offset their
negative impact. In chemistry, if I want to neutralize an
acid, I must counter with the equivalent of an opposite
substance. Forgiveness works like that. It's an alkaline
nullifying the acidic nature of bitterness. It's that balancing presence that says "You can remind me of my pain,
but you can't rob me of my rest."

If we don't deal with our unresolved conflicts, they'll
deal with us. Bitterness is a slavemaster. It controls us.
It demands too much.

The requirements for maintaining anger and resentment are steep. You've got to overtax friendships, ruin special events that could have become great memories, make your kid's lives miserable, get bad reviews at work for allowing your personal life to affect your job performance, prejudge new relationships, isolate yourself from people who need you, and neutralize the impact of God's Word in your life.

Bitterness affects us physically, too. It might reward us with a miserable night's sleep or an upset stomach. It might spoil our appetite or drive us to eat too much. The relationship between physical health and inner joy is obvious. The unresolved anger and hurt festering in some people's hearts is guaranteeing them a rough ride to the morgue. It also promises to get them there sooner.

It's easy to read what's on your mind at this moment. All I have to do is read my own. You're thinking of the pain that you've endured—pain that seems too intense to forgive. I know how you feel. I think of some of the people who have had fun at my expense, who have attempted to move up the career ladder by trying to climb over me and then kick me off. I think of friends who said they'd be there—and weren't. I've felt the cold stainless steel of betrayal slipping into my back. And I've experienced the empty feeling that overwhelms you when you realize the hand shoving it in is the hand of a friend.

I've had the same choices that face all people. I could be haunted and hounded by hurt, or I could forgive. If I make the choice to forgive, it is not because of some intrinsic good in me. I'm just as capable of revenge as the next guy. My decision to forgive is more motivated by need and desperation.

The Hill of Forgiveness

When the crimes against my heart seem unforgivable, I am compelled to take a walk up a hill. Hurting hearts all over the world have learned the power that is gained by taking this same walk. We may start in the outbacks of Rhodesia, the frozen tundra of Siberia, or the congested sidewalks of Manhattan. Regardless of where we start our trek, the paths merge at the base of the same hill. It's the Hill of Forgiveness that sits at the center of civilization. The ground at the top is level. The grass growing around the wooden beam with its cross-beam ripples in the fresh breeze of freedom. There's always room for anyone wanting help for their hurt.

The cross is the single most significant symbol of forgiveness in history. Made by men, used by God, it is the hallmark of man at his worst and God at His best.

God gifted man with keen intellect and abundant natural resources. He buried ore in the ground and stood timber in the forest. Man uncovered that ore. He melted and molded it into spikes. Man cut down that timber and shaped the wood into a cross. God met man on the Hill of Forgiveness. With divine strength, the Creator stooped to the anger of the created. With eternal love He allowed Himself to be wounded at the four extremities of the cross.

God paid for man with outstretched arms. He no longer hangs on the cross, but His arms are in the same position. Because of Him, I'm forgiven in spite of myself. He receives the guilty. He welcomes the wounded.

None of us deserve this kind of forgiveness. It's a gift. Once you've received it, it's impossible to remain the same.

Jesus asks us to follow His example. "He never answered back when insulted; when he suffered he did not threaten to get even; he left his case in the hands of God who always judges fairly" (1 Peter 2:23 TLB). He says that forgiveness should become a way of life, regardless of how unfair people may be to you. "Stop being mean, bad-tempered and angry. Quarreling, harsh words, and dislike of others should have no place in your lives. Instead, be kind to each other, tenderhearted, forgiving one another, just as God has forgiven you because you belong to Christ" (Ephesians 4:31-32 TLB).

We want rest. But it will cost us. The menu for rest lists a lot of variations of "humble pie." But if pride is going to hold us hostage, we'll find that we are our own worst enemy. Maybe now is a good time for you to do some serious inventory of your life. Are there people whom you need to forgive? Do yourself a favor. Give them something they don't deserve but desperately need. Give them the gift of forgiveness. It's a gift that, once given, offers something in return. Your spirit gets a rest.

My football coach used to say, "Gentlemen, it takes fewer muscles to smile than to frown. We are going to need all your energy to win. So don't waste it on anger or fear. Smile!"

That's sound advice, whether you're trying to win at a game that lasts an hour or a battle that lasts a lifetime.

CHAPTER 5

Living Within the Limits

WHEN you're raised in the country, hunting is just a natural part of growing up.

For years I enjoyed packing up my guns and some food to head off into the woods. Even more than the hunting itself, I enjoyed the way these trips always seemed to deepen my relationship with friends as we hunted during the day and talked late into the night around the campfire. When an old friend recently invited me to relive some of those days, I couldn't pass up the chance.

For several weeks before the trip, I had taken the time to upgrade some of my equipment and sight in my rifle. When the day came, I was ready for the hunt. What I wasn't ready for was what my close friend, Tom, shared with me the first night out on the trail.

I always enjoyed the time I spent with Tom. He had become a leader in his church and his warm and friendly manner had also taken him many steps along the path of business success. He had a lovely wife, and while I knew they had driven over some rocky roads in their marriage, things now seemed to be stable and growing. Tom's kids, two daughters and a son, were struggling in junior high and high school with the normal problems of peer pressure and acceptance.

As we rode back into the mountains, I could tell that something big was eating away at Tom's heart. His normal effervescent style was shrouded by an overwhelming inner hurt. Normally, Tom would attack problems with the same determination that had made him a success in business. Now, I saw him wrestling with something that seemed to have knocked him to the mat for the count.

Silence has a way of speaking for itself. All day and on into the evening, Tom let his lack of words shout out his inner restlessness. Finally, around the first night's campfire, he opened up.

The scenario Tom painted was annoyingly familiar. I'd heard it many times before in many other people's lives. But the details seemed such a contrast to the life that Tom and his wife lived and the beliefs they embraced.

His oldest daughter had become attached to a boy at school. Shortly after they started going together, they became sexually involved. Within two months, she was pregnant. Tom's wife discovered the truth when a packet from Planned Parenthood came in the mail addressed to her daughter. When confronted with it, the girl admitted she had requested it when she went to the clinic to find out if she was pregnant.

If we totaled up the number of girls who have gotten pregnant out of wedlock during the past two hundred years of our nation's history, the total would be in the millions. Countless parents through the years have faced the devastating news. Being a member of such a large fraternity of history, however, does not soften the severity of the blow to your heart when you discover it's *your* daughter.

Tom shared the humiliation he experienced when he realized that all of his teaching and example had been ignored. Years of spiritual training had been thrust aside. His stomach churned as he relived the emotional agony of knowing that the little girl he and his wife loved so much had made a choice that had permanently scarred her heart.

I'm frequently confronted with these problems in my ministry and have found that dwelling on the promiscuous act only makes matters worse. I worship a God of forgiveness and solutions, and at that moment in our conversation I was anxious to turn toward hope and healing.

I asked Tom what they had decided to do. Would they keep the baby, or put it up for adoption?

That's when he delivered the blow.

With the fire burning low, Tom paused for a long time before answering. And even when he spoke he wouldn't look me in the eye.

"We considered the alternatives, Tim. Weighed all the options." He took a deep breath. "We finally made an appointment with the abortion clinic. I took her down there myself."

I dropped the stick I'd been poking the coals with and stared at Tom. Except for the wind in the trees and the snapping of our fire it was quiet for a long time. I couldn't believe this was the same man who for years had been so outspoken against abortion. He and his wife had even volunteered at a crisis pregnancy center in his city.

Heartsick, I pressed him about the decision. Tom then made a statement that captured the essence of his problem . . . and the problem many others have in entering into genuine rest.

In a mechanical voice, he said "I know what I *believe*, Tim, but that's different than what I had to *do*. I had to make a decision that had the least amount of consequences for the people involved."

Just by the way he said it, I could tell my friend had rehearsed these lines over and over in his mind. And by the look in his eyes and the emptiness in his voice, I could tell his words sounded as hollow to him as they did to me.

In one sweeping statement, Tom had articulated a major trend that is robbing the American home of rest.

WHEN SITUATIONAL VALUES
PUSH ASIDE SCRIPTURAL BELIEFS

So many of the people approaching me for counseling want relief without reprimand. They want to find solutions to their inner restlessness, but don't want to change their lifestyle. They want to feel the peace of God while living in direct opposition to the stated principles of His Scriptures. In short, they want the freedom to live life outside the protective fence of God's Word—yet with the gate left open so they can rush back inside and avoid any negative consequences for their actions.

Let me list a few of the ways I've seen people trying to live on both sides of the fence:

—A service manager is outspoken about his desire to be a deacon at his church but is even more outspoken in his use of coarse language at work to "motivate" his men.

—A mother is addicted to the most permissive of the daytime soaps, but preaches to her daughter about the questionable messages of rock 'n' roll.

—An employee outfits his desk at home with supplies he requisitioned from work.

—A man goes on vacation with his family but makes one "business" call in order to deduct the entire trip on his income taxes.

—A mother reprimands her child for lying to her, but consistently has the same child tell a caller to whom she doesn't want to speak that she is "not home."

—A husband lectures his kids about their taste in movies, but rents adult videos for private viewing.

—A mom and dad drop the kids off at church while they slip away for some "needed time together" at a restaurant.

Whatever Happened to Right and Wrong?

A funny thing happened on the way to the twenty-first century. We decided that the concept of sin was something we should leave behind as archaic and out-of-date. While we were busy locating the elusive self inside of us, we decided that guilt was too painful. The only solution was to change the rules and "redefine" wrong.

Newsweek columnist Meg Greenfield had some interesting thoughts on this phenomenon in a piece entitled, "Why Nothing is Wrong Anymore." In our society, she suggested, the word "wrong" has been taken out of "right and wrong." What's been substituted? How about "right and stupid," "right and unconstitutional," or "right and emotionally ill"?[6]

Don't think her logic stops outside the front door of the Christian community. On the contrary, it comes right inside. Many Christians would change the couplet to read: "Right and what I *feel* is right."

In other words, let's skip over those tough sections of the Bible that talk about God's hatred for adultery and divorce in favor of sections filled with more "hope and compassion."

I think of people like Alice . . . who had read all the verses about not marrying a non-Christian, but did so anyway because "It can't be wrong when it feels so right." Their child is now suffering the abuse and neglect of an alcoholic dad.

I think of people like Chad . . . who met and married a woman on the same weekend his divorce came through because he felt God wanted him to—and that very weekend his former wife came looking for him to ask if he'd be willing to restore their relationship.

I think of people like Kyle . . . who volunteered his

time at a crisis pregnancy center to give unborn children the right to life—but didn't feel like allowing a pregnant daughter to live at home because of the negative affect it would have on his clients.

Where does the epidemic of hypocrisy and shifting standards leave us? Without exception, it leads us to the wilderness of unrest. How can we return to the place where right is right, and wrong is not excused on the basis of our feelings? By following a narrow way marked off by an eternal Book—a pathway that offers freedom and rest by giving us the choice to live life within the standards of God's word.

THE SECOND NECESSITY: WE MUST LIVE OUR LIVES WITHIN THE BOUNDARIES OF GOD'S WORD

Throughout Scripture and throughout the ages, those who have entered into God's rest have done so by making a conscious choice to stay within the protective fence of God's standards. Put another way, the further we walk away from biblical guidelines, the closer we get to the cliffs of anxiety, fear, worry, and unrest.

Back in 1967, one of my classmates in graduate school spent four harrowing months in Vietnam before being wounded and shipped home. One story he told taught me a lot about the urgency of staying within protective boundaries.

As the Vietnam war escalated, Mike knew that his chance of being drafted was high. With that fact staring him in the face, he decided to enlist. It was a good thing, because two days later he received his draft notice. *At least*, he told himself, *I'm going to get a preference of what branch and what unit I'm going to be in.*

Mike chose the artillery because he figured that if he did have to go to Nam, he would at least be behind the lines lobbing shells long-distance at the enemy. What he didn't know was that his choice would put him in some of the heaviest fighting of the war.

Following his training, he received orders to go overseas with a unit assigned to guard the perimeter of the Da Nang airbase. On the long plane flight to Vietnam, they were congratulating themselves on their good fortune of being stationed so far from the front lines. And while this proved true for many of the men, the first thing Mike found waiting for him at the airfield was a packet with "special" orders. He was to immediately join a convoy which took his field piece and four men over treacherous territory to a Green Beret camp . . . right on the very edge of no-man's-land.

The Special Forces stationed at this remote fire-base were weapons experts, skilled in search-and-destroy missions and hand-to-hand combat. Mike and his gun crew found themselves the only regular army soldiers in the middle of this elite fighting corps.

For nearly four months, Mike learned the life-saving nature of boundaries as two eight-foot barbed wire fences provided his greatest sense of protection. For almost a hundred yards outside the outermost fence, all the grass and trees had been cleared. Buried land mines and other anti-personnel ordnance hidden in this open area provided further protection for those within the compound.

There were trails through the mines that the Green Berets would use to come in and out from patrol. One afternoon a man under Mike's command ventured gingerly across one of those trails to pick some fruit in the nearby jungle.

Besides an occasional mortar shell falling near the perimeter, there had been no direct enemy attack since they had taken up their station. In fact, it had been over a week since his gun battery had been called on to provide supporting fire for one of the patrols. Even then it was for a unit near the limits of his range.

"Why can't we go outside the fence for awhile?" one of his gunners had asked him. "The Berets do it all the time . . ." Lounging near their cannon, the rest of the crew watched as this man headed out of the compound toward the fresh fruit that had tempted all of them since they arrived.

Mike's friend had nearly reached the edge of the forest when they saw him stop suddenly and take a step back. He turned suddenly and began to run back toward the fence. But out of the jungle came the sickening sounds of automatic rifle fire. The young man's body was shot to pieces before it ever hit the ground. In just moments, the quiet that had lasted for weeks was shattered by the scream of incoming mortar rounds. The attacking NVA troops poured out of the jungle like angry fire ants—many of them following the very route they had seen Mike's friend take through the minefield.

For three hours the fighting was intense—and often hand-to-hand. At one point, Mike ordered his cannon cranked down level, firing point-blank into the incoming troops. Somehow the men held their position. Mike and many others sustained severe wounds. Others hadn't been so fortunate.

As Mike related this story, he closed it with words that will always ring in my ears.

"Tim, you want to know why I don't fight God when it comes to areas he tells me in His Word to avoid? Because I've seen what it's like to walk outside the fence, and I don't want any part of it."

Whether we realize it or not, when we decide to walk away from God's Word and the clear boundaries it establishes for our lives, we are walking into no-man's land. While the danger we face will not be bullets or mortar fire, the spiritual flames and arrows of an unseen enemy can prove every bit as deadly. No piece of fruit, however tempting, is worth rendering ourselves defense-less and vulnerable by venturing outside the fence of His Word.

The Gift of Guilt

While we may never have thought of it this way before, one of the greatest gifts God has given us is the ability to experience and feel guilt. While Freud and others have called it the "universal neurosis"—a destruc-tive force in people's lives—it can actually be something God uses to protect us.

I'm not saying that all guilt is good. Imaginary guilt, or guilt imposed on us by people wanting to control us doesn't serve our best interests. Scripture tell us there is a sorrow that leads to death, but also speaks of a "sorrow that leads to repentance"(2 Corinthians 7:9-10) It's this second aspect of guilt that we need to make our ally, not our enemy.

Guilt serves us spiritually the way fever serves us physically. When we get a fever, our body is telling our mind that we have a sickness somewhere. A person who wants to get better doesn't ignore his symptoms. Neither does he hate himself because he's feeling sick. Rather, the negative feelings act as a physical reminder that the fence has been crossed between sickness and health.

In the same way, guilt tells us that something is wrong with us emotionally or spiritually. It says in a clear way, *You're stepping outside the fence by making this decision. . . pursuing this relationship . . . avoiding this person . . . accepting this invitation. . . .*

To use another analogy, guilt is like the oil light on the instrument panel of your life. When it comes on, it's saying "Hey, friend, check your life! You're headed for problems if you don't!" You can choose to ignore this spiritual warning light—you may even, by repeated sin-ning, sever the wires that connect it—but ultimately the consequence of your sin will bring your life to a screeching halt.

As we close this chapter, let me make two suggestions which can help you grab hold of this crucial element of rest. The first has to do with the subtle difference between "beliefs" and "values," and the second with the incredible impact living within the lines can have on your friends and loved ones.

COMING HOME TO GOD'S BOUNDARIES

For the past twenty years, our nation has been shifting from living according to beliefs to living according to "values." Let's define the difference.

A belief system answers the question, "What is right and what is wrong?" A value system answers the question, "What am I going to do?" Beliefs form the foundation on which we anchor our lives, and give us a clear standard to live by. Values, on the other hand, should be an *outgrowth* of our beliefs. Beliefs should represent our absolutes; values should represent the actions we take based on those beliefs.

For the Christian, there is another aspect thrown in. Instead of simply asking, "What is right and wrong?" we have been given guidelines in God's Word that call us to say, "Because of my belief in Christ, what is right and wrong?" Beliefs take their shape in that book which sits on our nightshelf or that we carry to church—the Scriptures. Values are those actions which should flow out of the beliefs we form based on His Word—a recognition that we are the Lord's and our lives are not our own. With this in mind, let's move from the theoretical to the practical.

To ignore or explain away our beliefs and then insist we still have "values" is like trying to wag a tail that is no longer attached to the cat. My friend Tom had an absolute understanding—a firm belief—on the sanctity of human life . . . until it inconvenienced him. Then he simply adjusted his values so that they were more comfortable to live with. He quit asking the question, "Based on the Scripture, what is right and wrong?" and simply stuck with the question, "What shall I do?" His values still had to have a base to stand on, only now instead of resting on God's word, they stood on shifting sand.

As a nation, we have dealt with difficult moral issues in much the same way my friend Tom dealt with his dilemma. Instead of holding firm to the bedrock biblical issues of right and wrong, we have simply "changed our minds" about whether something is right or wrong.

We used to be a nation largely opposed to gambling. Today, an increasing number of churches run bingo games, and most states run lotteries. Drinking was once frowned on. Today nearly two-thirds of Americans drink at least casually. Premarital sex was the exception in the past; now it's the rule. According to federal statistics, half of the women getting married during the 1960s had sex before marriage. Today, more than four out of five women getting married report they have had sexual experience.[7]

There is a crucial distinction about those statistics. Of the 50 percent of the women getting married in the 1960s who confessed to premarital sex, most of them would have admitted that their actions were "wrong." If you polled the 80 percent of women getting married today who admit to premarital sex, few of them would say they did anything wrong.

Once we left our belief system behind—what God's Word has clearly said about right and wrong—we also began turning down the volume on our conscience. And therein lies the greatest threat to rest in our home. *As we become more comfortable at having one standard for our spiritual destiny and another for our daily choices and actions, we complicate the task of parenting—and increase our personal level of restlessness.*

Here's the bottom line regarding the element of rest: We need to align our actions with our beliefs. In so doing, we acknowledge that there is a protective fence God has put around our behavior. We honor Him, we honor our loved ones, and we honor ourselves by respecting it. If we try to explain away its existence, we're going to trip headlong into a world of hurt.

If we haven't done so already, we need to ask ourselves a difficult question that demands an honest answer. Are there areas, responses, goals, relationships, or dreams in our life that we know, today, are outside the boundary of God's Word? To whatever degree we have walked outside the fence to embrace these things—no matter how attractive the fruit—we are, to that degree, preventing ourselves from experiencing genuine rest.

God promised to lead Joshua and the ancient nation of Israel to a place of rest. But along with the promise came a warning. "Be strong and very courageous. . . . Don't turn from [the law] to the right or to the left, that you may be successful wherever you go" (Joshua 1:7).

In some cases, staying within the fence of God's word is far more difficult than walking outside it—but our sleep will be sweeter and our life filled more fully with His rest. And that's not all. Our example of living life within the lines can lead others to find rest as well. Just as it did for one pastor several years ago.

Limits Which Provide Lessons

There was a pastor of a large congregation who preached a sermon on honesty at each of his church's three services one Sunday morning. The next day, with his car in the shop, he decided to use the local bus to get to his office.

He stepped up into the bus and handed the driver a five dollar bill. (This was several years ago and the words, "Exact change, please" had not yet been invented by bus drivers.) The driver took his money, gave him his ticket and a handful of bills for change.

When the pastor got to his seat and went to put the

change back in his wallet, he noticed that the driver had given him too much. For the duration of the bus trip, the pastor made every attempt to rationalize why he should keep the change. He thought, "Maybe God knew that I needed some extra money this week" or "I could give this extra money to God's service."

But his conscience wouldn't let him off. On his way out the door, he stopped and handed the money to the driver.

"I'm afraid you made a mistake," he said, "You've given me too much change."

The driver smiled, "There was no mistake, *pastor*. I was at your church yesterday and heard you preach on honesty. When you handed me that five, I thought I'd see if you were as good at practicing as you are at preaching!"

As the bus idled at the stop, the driver continued. "You know, Sunday was the first time I agreed to go to church with my wife. I've always thought you guys were a bunch of phonies, but I guess there's more to it than that. I'll see you *next* Sunday."

"No fair! Entrapment!" some might shout today. Yet this bus driver saw in real life that this pastor's beliefs and his actions corresponded—and it led him to a personal faith in Jesus Christ.

How about us? Are we experiencing the benefit of concrete beliefs and corresponding actions?

Husbands, like it or not, your wife is looking at you today and asking that question. Wives, it's being asked of you, too. Parents, get ready to be tested if you haven't been already. Children can sniff out hypocrisy like a pet duck can sniff out popcorn. And while we may put on a great front with those who don't know us as well at work or at church, this is the day of investigative reporting and "no holds barred" analysis. If what we say we believe isn't what we live, we don't have to be a political candidate to be found out.

We give our family and ourselves an incredible gift when we make the decision to live within God's limits. It opens the door to genuine rest in our lives, and perhaps even more importantly, it models the pathway to rest that they can follow in theirs.

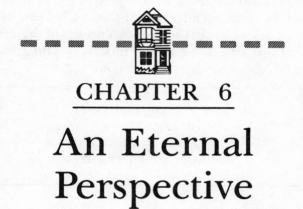

CHAPTER 6

An Eternal Perspective

MY wife and I view our children's bedtime as the most critical time of their daily routine (getting up is critical time number two). Before Mr. Sandman leans over the edge of their covers to sprinkle sleep dust into their eyes, we like to sprinkle some rest into their souls. Rest for their bodies prepares them for tomorrow, but rest for their souls prepares them for a lifetime. How we bring the daily clutter of events, emotions, and experiences to a conclusion has a big effect on how my children view themselves and the world in which they are attempting to live.

Darcy and I are painfully aware that these moments of closeness are passing. As we watch our children outgrow favorite toys, favorite songs, and favorite pillows, we know they must soon outgrow this little bedtime ritual as well. Sooner than we think, children are too big to rock to sleep. So these special times of reflection and perspective must not be taken lightly. The calmness of spirit passed on to our children must serve them in the darkest hours of their lives.

That's why I like to use the final conversations of the day to emphasize the third necessity for genuine rest. It's the one that most affects their choices. If I can implant this one perspective in the deepest crevices of their young minds, I can save them a lot of mistakes—and give their spirits a consistent sense of freedom.

THE THIRD NECESSITY:
EVERYDAY LIFE MUST ALWAYS
BE LIVED AGAINST THE
BACKDROP OF ETERNITY

Everything in life takes on a different perspective when weighed against eternity. Relationships, accomplishments, and disappointments assume significant new meanings. It is essential that my children learn to factor in the eternal as they calculate the meaning of various circumstances that blend together in the formula of life.

The purpose is neither to spoil the joy of a victory, nor to soften the seriousness of a defeat. Life is both temporal *and* eternal. The day to day events that bring wrinkles to our foreheads, smiles to our faces, or tears to our eyes have a right to an immediate response. Whether we skin our knees, wound our spirits, or break our hearts, the emotions of the moment need to be felt. It would be wrong to deny them expression.

Winning the Little League championship calls for a celebration, and being cut from this year's cheerleading squad might require sackcloth and ashes. Nothing is gained by reminding your son that "as far as eternity goes, the outcome of the game is meaningless." Nor does the counsel that "when you're dead and gone no one will remember who was on the cheerleading squad anyway" do anything but demonstrate an appalling lack of sensitivity.

An absurd preoccupation with the "sweet by and by" makes us of little value to people living in the "nasty now and now." Nonetheless, *we are eternal people*. Because we are, it would be equally absurd to ignore the obvious impact of our eternal nature. True, planet earth logs time in hours, minutes, and seconds. And the tombstones that checker the cemeteries of the world have two dates under each name. But it is easy to forget that time is only relevant to our physical body. The soul that shares the body lives beyond the tomb. Its eternal destination has a timely influence on our day to day perspective.

There's that word again.

So much of the key to rest is wrapped up in our *perspective*. That's why seeing ourselves against an eternal backdrop is so critical. If forgiveness gives us the ability to love, and clear boundaries a crystallized purpose, an eternal perspective gives us hope.

Again, that's the reason I like to throw the experiences of the day up against the infinite backdrop of God's plan. As we review our children's day and note the highlights as well as try to give wise counsel about the low spots, we also try to remind them of their eternal legacy. They need to know that they are not chance happenings on a planet with no purpose.

Today was no accident. Tomorrow is part of forever.

THE SECURITY OF THE ETERNAL

I'm amazed how many people get tripped up on this issue. So many of the disappointments in people's lives come because they fail to factor in the eternal. Without a regular reminder that "This world is not my home, I'm just passing through," it's hard to enjoy contentment. We are forced to evaluate everything happening to us by arbitrary and superficial standards. Self-worth becomes an issue of achievement. Satisfaction becomes an issue of acquisition. Without the eternal, I'm in competition with the best the world can put forth rather than the best that lies within me. If I'm not feeling pushed by the competition breathing down my neck, I feel pulled by those way out ahead of me.

Life without an eternal perspective trades living for longing, exchanges happiness for hurriedness, and gives up rest for restlessness. When this life is all that we've got going for us, we're forced to grab all the gusto we can. As fast as we can.

But once upon a time, an eternal God decided to give man a rest. It was an invitation to slow down and last longer. The price tag was high, but the end result was worth it for Him. He gave up something in order to win. He knew that living would first require dying, but that death would be the Gateway to Eternity.

So the God who once slept in a manger climbed up on a cross. He paid the price for inner rest. He took the shame, the guilt, and the punishment for our sins. He took care of the one problem that all men share in common—their lost condition.

But His Word makes it clear that dying wasn't enough. On Sunday morning when the stone that sealed Jesus in His crypt was supernaturally rolled back, the morning light crept across the floor and up the ledge to a pile of graveclothes. Jesus had carefully folded the turban that had concealed His death face and placed it where his lifeless head once lay.

Jesus vacated the grave in order to invade our hearts. Without the resurrection of Christ, there is only man-made hope. When Paul addressed this issue, he recognized how genuine hope pivoted on the certainty that Christ deserted the grave.

> If only for this life we have hope in Christ, we are to be pitied more than all men (1 Corinthians 15:19).

The message of the cross takes us beyond this life to eternal life. Those who embrace this truth are given the assurance that life on earth is just the beginning—a dress rehearsal.

The best is yet to come.

An Eternal Perspective Changes the Way We View People

If the best is yet to come, then we need to be careful about how we treat people. There is nothing more important than human beings. It's more than an issue of the sanctity of life. It's the reality that every person who walks on planet earth embodies a human spirit that lives forever. No other created thing can make that claim. Without a regular reminder that we are eternal, we could easily be drawn into the snare of prioritizing "things" over people. It's an easy trap to fall into—and has a lot to do with the volatile nature of relationships.

Relationships are risky. They have the power to make us or break us at a moment's notice. Even the most secure and balanced person is affected. Relationships become a guarded game of one-upmanship and "keeping the other guy off balance." We protect our intimate associations and are careful not to let too many people get close to us.

Things, on the other hand, seem more secure and become an attractive substitute for intimacy. They reward our egos and placate our consciences. We can surround ourselves with trophies. We can entertain ourselves to death with expensive, adult toys. We can even be applauded for community service that raises money for faceless people on the wrong side of the tracks. As long as we don't have to personally hold the cup of cold water as they're drinking from it, we're fine.

We can build a financial empire at the expense of our families and soothe our guilty spirits with rationalizations. "It's good for the economy." "It gave a lot of people jobs." "It provided my family with a better standard of living." There is no end to the ways we attempt to justify wrong priorities. But the fact is, we were designed to find completion in relationships—*not* in material possessions.

When we allow anything to undermine our responsibilities to others, we find a growing emptiness in our hearts. That's because, like it or not, we can't make it without relationships.

What we need is the ability to make choices that don't jeopardize eternal relationships for temporary rewards. An eternal perspective helps us do that. Those who recognize that relationships are more important than personal gain or personal satisfaction have a better chance of maintaining a rested spirit. They run their daily decisions through a grid that would never allow something that lasts for a moment (or even a lifetime) to take priority over a person who lasts forever.

My wife and I cling to a simple decision-making principle, an elementary rule of thumb that has kept us from veering off course again and again. It's given us a deep-seated confidence when we've faced tough choices about our kids, our friends, and each other. The principle is simply this: *NEVER SACRIFICE THE PERMANENT ON THE ALTAR OF THE IMMEDIATE.**

There are few guarantees in life. But I can guarantee you that making choices according to this principle can help keep you from neglecting the priority of people. It all hinges on an eternal perspective.

An Eternal Perspective Changes the Way We View Love

Knowing there's more to life than life on earth changes the way we view love. It can't be taken lightly. The people who represent the crucial relationships in our lives must be constantly viewed according to their eternal potential. Their destiny is contingent on their

---

* A speaker, Bob Krayning, from Forest Home shared this principle. It's some of the best counsel I've ever received.

response to God's work on the cross. I must take care, therefore, to never undermine their attitude toward God by taking a passive attitude toward my commitments to them.

Love is eternal. Although the marriage vows are confined to time, love isn't. Although death will someday separate me from my wife, we will meet again in heaven. Friends who embrace Christ for their salvation need to be viewed as *eternal* friends.

I picked up a collection of the works of Edgar Allan Poe not long ago and read my six-year-old daughter Karis some of his poems about love.

My favorite was her favorite . . . "Annabel Lee." She enjoyed it so much that she asked me to help her commit it to memory. In the days that followed, I reviewed it with her until she had it word perfect. If you recall the poem, Annabel Lee was a young girl whom Poe loved. But she came down with pneumonia and died before they were able to be married. The poem talks about love that is not able to be consumed by death.

> It was many and many a year ago,
>   In a kingdom by the sea,
> That a maiden there lived whom you may know
>   By the name of Annabel Lee;—
> And this maiden she lived with no other thought
>   Than to love and be loved by me.
>
> She was a child and I was a child,
>   In this kingdom by the sea,
> But we loved with a love that was more than love—
>   I and my Annabel Lee—
> With a love that the winged seraphs of Heaven
>   Coveted her and me.
>
> And this was the reason that, long ago,
>   In this kingdom by the sea,
> A wind blew out of a cloud by night
>   Chilling my Annabel Lee;

So that her highborn kinsmen came
    And bore her away from me,
To shut her up in a sepulchre
    In this kingdom by the sea.

The angels, not half so happy in Heaven,
    Went envying her and me;—
Yes! that was the reason (as all men know,
    In this kingdom by the sea)
That the wind came out of the cloud, chilling,
    And killing my Annabel Lee.

But our love it was stronger by far than the love
    Of those who were older than we—
    Of many far wiser than we—
And neither the angels in Heaven above,
    Nor the demons down under the sea,
Can ever dissever my soul from the soul
    Of the beautiful Annabel Lee:—

For the moon never beams without bringing me dreams
    Of the beautiful Annabel Lee;
And the stars never rise but I feel the bright eyes
    Of the beautiful Annabel Lee;
And so, all the night-tide, I lie down by the side
Of my darling, my darling, my life and my bride,
    In her sepulchre there by the sea—
    In her tomb by the side of the sea.

After reading the poem together, Karis and I had one of the best conversations about time and eternity we had ever had. It was an opportunity to review with her again the truth that *love isn't confined to time*. I want her to view the people she loves from an eternal perspective. That understanding can medicate her heart when it gets broken. When she loses someone she dearly loves, there will still be reasons to smile.

My mother died when I was thirty-four. I could go into a moving eulogy about what a great woman she was, but she wouldn't have preferred that. Mom made a quiet yet bold statement about God in the way that she loved my father, loved us kids, and cared for people. For her, human legacies were the only kind worth leaving.

At her funeral some well-meaning people tried to comfort me with worn out cliches. The bromide most frequently whispered in my ear was: "Time heals all wounds." It's now been several years since we buried Mom . . . and the pain of missing her is as fresh today as it was when I watched them lower her casket into the ground. Time *doesn't* heal all wounds. But when you love someone, it doesn't *have* to! The pain of missing Mom is a reminder of how special she was. It's a pain that puts a smile on my face.

An Eternal Perspective Changes the Way We View Death

Maintaining an eternal perspective helps us avoid a morbid preoccupation with death. Death doesn't have to loom on the horizon of our life as a vicious thief. It can be accepted in a healthy way as one of the necessary parts of life's formula.

My mother was diagnosed as terminally ill with cancer a few months before she died. The hospice program at the clinic she was confined to did a lot to help her and my family walk through the "valley of the shadow." I was reading one of their brochures in her room one day. Life, it said, is a process made up of three parts: you are born, you live, and you die. Healthy people are those who learn to accept death as a part of life.

That's fine, I thought, *except you forgot something. You're born, you live, you die, and then you live forever!* That's why King David referred to it as the "valley of the *shadow* of death" and not the "valley of death."

Shadows can't hurt me. What cast the shadow can. But God challenged death to a duel. Death chose a cross as its weapon. God fired back with an empty grave. He defeated death when He walked out of its grip into the light of a beautiful Sunday morning. For those who trust in this truth, it's eternally Sunday. That's why David could respond to the shadows of death that crossed his path with the words, "I fear no evil."

The job description of the Christian life is to be prepared to die at a moment's notice. God has taken the sting out of the process through the cross.

And once we are prepared to die, we are free to live.

An Eternal Perspective Changes the Way We View Aging

Have you ever noticed how the gravitational pull of the earth increases once you hit thirty? It's amazing how these bodies that once climbed mountains without working up a sweat need jump-starting to move from the dinner table to the Lazy-Boy recliner. I'm not ready to roll over and die, but I do find the process of staying in shape and feeling healthy requires a deliberate choice. (It's the human dilemma called, "The end doesn't justify the jeans.")

I like to get up every morning and run. Correction: I like to get up every morning. I *choose* to run. It's the lesser of the evils that face me as I move my way into the uncharted regions of middle age. I could let myself go to seed (which sounds like a lot more fun), or I can try to make the last half of my life as free of health problems as possible. That's why I get up and run.

There is a phenomenon in running called "hitting the wall." It's the invisible barrier that suddenly slows you down and tells you to quit. It's usually waiting for me *at the corner of my property*. I have to give myself quite a sermon to get past the first hundred feet. After that, the next few miles come easily.

I'm glad I don't have to determine my value in life by how well I keep up with the models waltzing down the fashion runways of Madison Avenue. Realizing that I am eternal has taken the threat out of aging. Planet earth possesses no fountain of youth. So I do the best I can with the health that I have, and accept, without threat, the inevitable effects of time.

I'll take it one step further: I'm convinced that an eternal perspective is the only thing that can give us the ability to actually *look forward* to growing old. Sure, there are liabilities. That's obvious. But there are assets that can offset them. Maturity steps in where youth steps out. Knowledge makes way for wisdom. Time becomes the valuable commodity it should have been from the beginning. And relationships become our life.

I should also mention that you finally get offspring that you get along with—grandchildren. The reason that grandparents bond so well with their grandchildren is because they share a common enemy.

Regardless, it isn't so bad growing old when you know that death isn't a period at the end of your life, but a comma separating the good from the best.

We have a cassette tape in our car that my whole family enjoys listening to. There is one song on it we fast-forward to over and over again. It's a piece by Steve and Annie Chapman called "The Seasons of a Man." It's one of the best songs I've heard that deals with the process of aging. It's also a great tool for keeping an eternal perspective in the minds of my kids.

In the first verse the voice of a little boy comes on singing about the first season.

> I am the springtime, when everything seems so fine.
> Whether rain or sunshine, you will find me playing.
> Days full of pretending.
> When a dime is a lot to be spending.
> A time when life is beginning.
> I am the springtime.

He is followed by an adolescent voice that sings about his season.

I am the summer. When the days are warm and longer.
When the call comes to wander, but I can't go far from home.
When the girls become a mystery.
When you're barely passing history.
And thinking old is when you're thirty.
I am the summer.

A voice of a man in his late thirties or early forties sings next.

And I am the autumn days. When changes come so many ways.
Looking back I stand amazed that time has gone so quickly.
When love is more than feelings.
It's fixing bikes and painting ceilings.
It's when you feel a cold wind coming.
I am the autumn days.

The last voice sounds stooped and tired. But it sings with an air of eternal wisdom and confidence.

I am the winter. When days are cold and bitter.
And the days I can remember number more than the days to come.
When you ride, instead of walking.
When you barely hear the talking.
And goodbyes are said too often.
I am the winter . . .
But I'll see springtime in heaven,
and it will last forever.[8]

An Eternal Perspective Changes the Way We View Time

Time is a *commodity*. A fixed number of days consumed but not replenished. It is the constant ticking on our wrist or the numbers that silently stare at us from our clock radio during a sleepless night. We block it into neat little days, stack them on top of each other, and call them months. We attach a pretty picture to the stack and package it as a calendar. But it's always moving. Racing forward. Ready or not. There it goes.

Time is a *process*. It's a homemade growth chart penciled on the doorjamb of the kitchen. It's boxes of neatly folded baby clothes stored in the toolshed. It's yearbooks with personal, handwritten notes from people you don't remember. It's when you no longer care whether you win or lose, but *how* you play the game.

Time is an *effect*. "Gee, Daddy, your hair is getting a lot grayer." "This belt's too small!" "I set out to do ten pushups but couldn't remember what number I was on." It's when you no longer care whether you win or lose, but *if* you can play the game.

How we view our time has everything to do with our ability to enjoy genuine rest. An eternal perspective helps us see time as a gift to be given to others, a precious investment in people who will live forever.

Perhaps you've run across the following story of a father and son who took two different views toward the proper use of time. They had the same last name and some similar physical characteristics, but other than that they were as different as the night is from the day.

They farmed a little piece of land, and a couple times a year they would set out with their wagon filled with vegetables for the market in a nearby city. The father set a modest pace leading the ox as the son sat fidgeting on the seat.

"Dad, we need to hurry so we can make it to town by tonight. We've got to set up early enough to get the best prices."

"Don't worry, son, we'll get there soon enough."

After an hour and a half of watching his father casually walking beside the beast, the younger man insisted on taking his turn at leading. The father lay down on the seat to take a nap as the son started poking the ox with a stick and harassing him to pick up his gait. The father peered out from under his hat at his impatient boy.

"Take your time son. You'll last longer."

The determined boy just shook his head in disgust. He swatted the ox's back with a vengeance.

Several hours later the father sat up and stretched.

"Look son, my brother's house. Pull in so I can visit him. We live so close but see each other so little."

"Father, we don't have the time!"

"What do you mean? All we have is time. That's why I want to use some of it talking to him."

The two men visited and laughed while the son paced. After an hour the father and son were back on the road. The father was leading when they came to a fork in the road. He nudged the ox to the right.

"The path to the left is quicker!"

"But this way is prettier, son."

"Have you no respect for time?"

"I certainly do. That's why I like to spend it looking at beautiful things."

The young man pulled his hat down over his eyes, crossed his arms, sat back in the seat, and tapped his nervous foot against the harness. He was so busy stewing that he failed to see the beautiful garden of flowers that blanketed both sides of the path.

Toward dark the father pulled over the wagon and started to unharness the ox for the night. The son didn't hide his anger.

"This is the last time I make this trip with you! If we had followed my plan we would have been there by now. We could have been set up for tomorrow's buyers and been sold out by noon. You're more interested in *flowers* than in making money!"

"Why, that's the nicest thing you've ever said to me!"

With that statement the father found a comfortable spot to lie down and was quickly asleep.

At dawn the son had the ox harnessed and his sleepy

father in the seat. After an hour or so they came on a man whose wagon was stuck in a ditch.

"Let's help him, son."

"And lose more time!"

"Nonsense. You may be in a ditch someday."

They helped the man out, and then started back on the path. It was about eight o'clock. Up ahead a flash of lightning crossed the sky, the thunder rolled off in the distance, and the skies turned black.

"Looks like the city is getting quite a storm."

"If we had been there, we would have had enough of our produce sold by now to not have to worry about the storm."

"Take your time, you'll last longer."

It wasn't until late in the afternoon that they reached the bluff overlooking the city. They both stared down at it for a long time without speaking. Finally the son looked at the father.

"I see what you mean, Dad."

And they both turned their cart around and walked away from what had once been the city of Hiroshima.

CHAPTER 7

Serving While Suffering

MILLIONS of Americans start their day the same way. Their rooster is a favorite disc jockey or a top forty tune. They grab a quick shower, take a few bites of a breakfast that comes from a box via the toaster, gulp down a microwaved cup of coffee, and exchange a quick kiss with their spouses as they jump into separate cars. A push of a button sends a silent signal to a mechanical muscle that lifts the garage door out of their way. The god of the rat race gives the inaudible command: "Start your engines!"

Thousands of cars from one suburb merge with thousands of cars from other suburbs on the eight-lane drag strips that link the bedroom with the board room.

It's the human race running in the human race.

The freeway has to be one of the most vivid illustrations of modern life imaginable. It can, at any given moment, express the heart and soul of a culture because it has, at any given moment, a complete representation of every strata of people.

The freeway is no respecter of persons. It doesn't discriminate according to age, gender, race, religion, or net worth. It's an asphalt artery carrying the rich and poor, the old and young, the winners and losers, the bold and the broken. It's a collection of people trying to keep up with the posted speed limit, and still arrive at their next opportunity in life a little sooner.

But there is a category of people on the freeway who do not represent the rank and file of life. Though they would *like* to be a part of the mainstream, factors beyond their control hold them back. You notice them out of your peripheral vision as you speed by. Some of them are broken down on the shoulder of the freeway. Others wait anxiously by emergency call boxes.

Who are these people who have been bumped out of life's mainstream? They are the people around us who suffer. I've observed four types of sufferers parked alongside the freeway. I call them THE BEWILDERED, THE BADGERED, THE BATTERED, and THE BRO-KEN. Although their frustrations may have nothing in common, the effect of their frustrations is the same.

I've made two observations about people who suffer. First, of all the deterrents to experiencing genuine rest, there is nothing that can drain it away faster than suffering. Second, suffering people who are willing to bring rest to their lives enjoy *a richer and better degree of rest* than those who rest without suffering.

If you'll allow me to carry this analogy of a freeway a bit further, I'm sure you'll see my point.

Those Who Are Bewildered

The Portland *Oregonian* recently carried the tragic account of an elderly couple from British Columbia who became disoriented while driving their motor home through Portland. They had a reservation at a local motel, but couldn't seem to locate it in the city's maze of bridges, ramps, and crisscrossing freeways. An unidentified man apparently saw them on a shoulder of the road consulting a city map. He pulled his own car over and asked if he could help.

Perhaps the older lady, who was driving, couldn't understand his directions. That was why the man evidently suggested that the bewildered couple simply follow his car and he would lead them to their destination.

It sounded like such a good idea. But something went wrong. In her anxiety to keep up with the man's car, the old lady failed to negotiate a turn and plunged the vehicle through a guardrail. The motorhome flipped in the air and crashed upside down on the freeway some forty feet below. The woman died instantly, the man enroute to the hospital. The would-be guide slammed on his brakes, observed the carnage below, then sped away before police could arrive on the scene.

We've all found ourselves disoriented from time to time.

Getting lost on the freeways of contemporary culture isn't that hard to do. With our rush hour lifestyles and passing lane mentalities it's usually just a matter of time before we find ourselves moving with the flow . . . but not sure where we are.

Sometimes it's a case of not knowing where we're going. But I think that's usually the exception. Most often we know where we want to be, we're just not quite sure how to *get* there. And we're certain that we don't want to be where we are.

In my line of work, I meet a lot of people who are confused. They are confused because people keep changing the rules. They are confused because they've been handed inaccurate road maps through life. They are confused because people they think should be "reliable" keep giving them wrong directions.

They may believe the truth of the Bible, but they've been given so much conflicting counsel that they've lost all sense of direction. *Rest?* It's out of the question, as anyone who has ever found himself lost or disoriented for any length of time will quickly agree.

Some three thousand years ago, Isaiah spoke of the highwaymen who control you by keeping you confused. He wrote,

> Woe to those who call evil good, and good evil; who substitute darkness for light and light for darkness; who substitute bitter for sweet, and sweet for bitter! Woe to those who are wise in their own eyes, and clever in their own sight! (Isaiah 5:20-21 NAS).

Some good people get turned around on their way to contentment. Some of the wrong directions and misplaced road signs go something like this:

> there is no way that God ever intended any of His children to be poor or sick

> success is the only accurate way of measuring your true worth

> the top of the corporate ladder is the only place worth ending up

> don't let your family rob you of your big opportunity

> there are some sins your spouse can commit that are simply unforgivable

> you don't have to wait until you are making more money to enjoy your dream home now

Most people succumb to these confusing signals because they stop submitting to the only universally reliable road map through life—the Bible. G. K. Chesterton said, "When man declares that there is no God, instead of believing in nothing, he'll believe in anything." I think that can happen even if you still believe in God. All you have to do is stop depending on His day to day guidance.

Although I believe in individual responsibility for one's actions, I can't help but feel that some of these folks who have lost their way are victims. They listened to the eloquent and well-dressed charlatans who maintain such an effective throat-hold on this generation. Before they knew it, they'd been misled.

I know their plight. I've been misled. I've been confused. You have every confidence that you're doing well, heading in the right direction, then you look around and realize you're way off course. Until you find your way back to the right highway, your life is filled with restless frustration.

Those Who Are Badgered

It's never happened to me, but I've seen it happen to others. Some guy with a chip on his shoulder gets in his car under the illusion that the government built the entire freeway system for his private use. He pulls down the on-ramp and proceeds to control all three lanes through the twentieth-century art of auto intimidation.

He's angry. But the object of his anger isn't there to kick around, so he takes it out on the little people. As long as there are people, there will be bullies. But unchecked bullies can destroy a lot of lives before someone gets them under control. It's hard to take in the scenery when he's wanting to occupy the same spot in the road as you.

I've seen people forced to swerve into traffic to avoid them. I've seen the bullies slow down to give a senior citizen a piece of their angry mind. I've seen the road hogs threaten a mother with a car full of kids. You want to do something, but there's nothing you can do. The people who spend a lot of their time badgering others do their damage before you can get to them.

There is an obvious analogy between being badgered on the highways and being badgered in your day to day life.

Maybe it's the qualified employee who deserves the promotion but is passed up because the manager wanted his pet or "yes man" to have the position.

Maybe it's the neighborhood bully who keeps intimidating your kid while his father cheers him on.

Maybe it's the church gossip who won't let your past lie at the foot of the cross where you left it.

Maybe it's the tape of your father's voice that plays over and over inside your head, "You're stupid, and you'll never amount to anything."

Maybe it's the former spouse who is committed to destroying your new marriage.

Maybe it's the wayward son who keeps dragging you from the principal's office to juvenile court.

It doesn't take much badgering before you start to feel helpless. At that point, a rested spirit is as far from your mind as it can be.

The things (or people) which badger our lives don't have to be bigger, stronger, or more influential than us. They just have to be persistent.

There is a United States postal worker who learned this in an unfortunate way. It seems that he was severely bitten by a dog belonging to a lonely and angry lady. Because of the extent of his wounds, the law required the dog to be destroyed. That was when the undeclared war began.

The lady's heart filled with rage. She decided that if she could not have her dog, then this man and his family would not have another day's rest "as long as she lived."

She called him all hours of the night. Whoever answered the phone would be treated to an unsolicited tirade accented with the vilest obscenities. It didn't matter whether it was his youngest child or his wife, the message was the same.

Naturally he changed his phone number. She found out what it was. He got an unlisted number. Her network of spies found that number. When she couldn't get him through the telephone, she used an even better form of communication—the gossip chains. She passed lies that couldn't help but discredit the man as a father and a government worker.

The man was forced to put his house up for sale and relocate in order to get peace. Before that happened a judge of the court said enough is enough. He made it clear to the lady that even though she was over seventy years old, he would not hesitate to incarcerate her (without a phone), if she didn't bring her behavior to a halt. She called the judge's bluff and he played his hand. He sent her to jail for thirty days. It's hard to believe, but she even tried the same trick from the phone at the jail.

What do you do when the only thing keeping someone alive is the joy they receive from hating you? How can you find rest when restlessness stalks you and hounds you every waking moment of your day?

Those Who Are Broken

Our culture is directly responsible for the traffic reporter. People in a hurry listen to them religiously. They warn us where the major traffic arteries have become snarled. They suggest alternative routes and escape options that will save us time. They keep our impatient spirits from exploding.

The main problem they report is stalled or stranded vehicles. We've all experienced the frustration that builds inside when we sit in the middle of a bottleneck caused by a motorist with a flat tire or overheated radiator. It burns us to think one guy could hold up so many people.

Some people's cars break down because they fail to maintain them. They are probably getting what they asked for. But cars are machines, and even the best maintained machine will break down occasionally. Cars fresh off the showroom floor or straight from the mechanic's garage have failed in traffic. But when the average person is inconvenienced by them, he finds it hard to be patient. His emotions go in one of two directions. He's either annoyed that he's been held up, or he's glad that it happened to somebody else and not to him.

There is a whole group of people stranded on the side of life's road who receive a similar response from the people in the fast lane. For these people, the inequities of life cause them to be the true sufferers.

The obvious members of this category are the physically handicapped. The wheelchair user, the blind, and the deaf have so much to offer but are often denied by a system that takes survival of the fittest to a ridiculous extreme. Because these examples are the extreme forms of physical handicap we tend to think of them first. But there are a host of other sufferers who occupy a stranded position on the shoulders of the fast lane.

Arthritics, terminal patients, those who suffer from cluster headaches and PMS, and those with speech impediments are just a few examples of the kind of people who are forced to live in a society that isn't very sympathetic to their problems.

There are two other groups of people who can find themselves sidelined simply because they are the "wrong" age. Children and senior citizens do not fit very well into the hurried lifestyle. When society doesn't want to accommodate them, they are often forced over to the side of the shoulder where they watch life go by without them.

If you feel like you are one of these broken people, rest is probably hard for you to enjoy.

Those Who Are Battered

One of the most terrifying experiences of life is to be in a car accident. At the instant of impact lives can be permanently changed. Some accidents are nobody's fault. The damages may be severe, but the fact that it was unavoidable and no one was to blame makes coping a little easier.

But what about those collisions that were the result of someone else's irresponsibility? They cut the heart out of your joy. They cause a suffering that sometimes plagues you for life.

But we all know there are other crashes. Terrible, silent collisions that never show up in the newspaper's accident reports. Battered men and women who face staggering emotional pain . . . victims who must learn to live with a permanently injured life.

> the father who comes home to a full house, but an empty bedroom. His wife didn't say where she was going, just that she would never be back.

> the parents who found their daughter's body next to the suicide note.

> the fifty-year-old employee who faithfully served his company but is out of a job because the company that purchased his company decided to eliminate an entire level of management.

Sometimes the only mistake you made was being born into the wrong family. But that single unfortunate dilemma can cost you forever.

Take Edwin Thomas, for instance. Edwin Thomas Booth, that is. At age fifteen he debuted on the stage playing Tressel to his father's Richard III. Within a few short years he was playing the lead in Shakespearean tragedies throughout the United States and Europe. He was the Olivier of his time. He brought a spirit to tragedy that put him in a class by himself.

Edwin had a younger brother, John, who was also an actor. Although he could not compare with his older brother, he did give a memorable interpretation of Brutus in the 1863 production of *Julius Caesar*, by the New York Winter Garden Theater. Two years later, he performed his last role in a theater when he jumped from the box of a bloodied President Lincoln to the stage of Ford's Theater. John Wilkes Booth met the end he deserved. But his murderous life placed a stigma over the life of his brother Edwin.

An invisible asterisk now stood beside his name in the minds of the people. He was no longer Edwin Booth the consummate tragedian, but Edwin Booth the brother of the assassin. He retired from the stage to ponder the question *why?*

Edwin Booth's life was a tragic accident simply because of his last name. The sensationalists wouldn't let him separate himself from the crime.

It is interesting to note that he carried a letter with him that could have vindicated him from the sibling attachment to John Wilkes Booth. It was a letter from General Adams Budeau, Chief Secretary to General Ulysses S. Grant, thanking him for a singular act of bravery. It seems that while he was waiting for a train on the platform at Jersey City, a coach he was about to board bolted forward. He turned in time to see that a young boy had slipped from the edge of the pressing crowd into the path of the oncoming train. Without thinking, Edwin raced to the edge of the platform and, linking his leg around a railing, grabbed the boy by the collar. The grateful boy recognized him, but he didn't recognize the boy. It wasn't until he received the letter of thanks that he learned it was Robert Todd Lincoln, the son of his brother's future victim.[9]

Tragedy wrings rest from our spirits. It did for Edwin Booth, and maybe it has for you. You may be bewildered, badgered, broken, or battered. If you are, then you need the message that makes up the fourth principle of genuine rest.

**THE FOURTH NECESSITY:
ACCEPTING AND SERVING
ARE THE BEST ANTIDOTES FOR
SUFFERING**

Suffering can cause us to turn our backs on the first three necessities for rest. It challenges our willingness to forgive. It tempts us to rationalize our wrong behavior. It so absorbs us that it's difficult to see past today. The fourth necessity for rest can counter the effects of suffering. I use as my defense the one person who "was tested in all points just as we are, yet without sin."

Jesus was bewildered. God bewildered? The God side of the Godman was never bewildered. But the humanity of Jesus felt the frustration of having to deal with inconsistent disciples, hypocritical religious leaders, and a divine plan to save man that required his impending death.

Jesus was badgered. From the outset of His ministry, Jesus was the object of public scorn. The religious leaders who should have welcomed Him with open arms led the chants against Him.

Jesus was broken. The Man of Sorrows broke down in a quiet corner of a city park. The blood that seeped from His sweat glands hinted at the extent of His anguish.

Jesus was battered. Sin, death, and Satan attacked Him at the cross. The holes they drilled into His hands and feet, and the spear wound in his side were only the outward signs of an internal hurt. The God of Abraham, Isaac, and Jacob came to give his life for His enemies. He did it so that they could become His friends.

There are two actions that Jesus took to counter the effects of the restless and ruthless world He came to save.

These are the same solutions that can help bring rest back to your suffering spirit.

The Solution of Acceptance

When an individual finds himself having to endure some discomfort or severe suffering, it's easy for him to go to one of two extremes. He either denies that it could actually be happening to him, or he assumes that God is going to intervene in some supernatural way and make the pain go away.

God *is* a God of miracles. He performs them all the time. But there is a difference between a God of miracles and a God of *magic*. Miracles are done for His glory, magic is performed for our entertainment. The normal human response to suffering is a plea to take it away. But God isn't required to do it, nor is it His standard way of handling our problems.

To deny the reality of our suffering is unhealthy. Imagine that your company lays you off at age fifty from a high paying job and you can't get work anywhere because you're too old. It might be a temptation to think that you are going to wake up one morning and find they are inviting you back to head the company. It might be a temptation to fantasize that other companies are going to suddenly change their views about hiring older men. But my observations tell me it's unlikely you'll be able to enjoy inner rest with that attitude.

You might find out that you have a debilitating disease. God could miraculously heal you. But what if He chooses not to? You could be living with an alcoholic. You could deny that he is an alcoholic. You could believe that God is going to intervene and take away his craving for alcohol. You can believe that real life stories have fairy-tale endings. But a *more biblical approach* is to *accept* the obvious and the inevitable.

Jesus knew that He was heading for a cross from the time He was born. During His three-year public ministry, He alluded several times to His ultimate destiny. But as He got closer, the human nature that hurts and feels rejection surfaced. At one point He fell on His face pleading with His Father to see if there was any way that "this cup could pass" from Him. He loved lost men, and was committed to obeying His Father, but like any person with human feelings, He wanted to avoid the excruciating suffering that was awaiting Him on the cross.

An interesting thing happened once He accepted the inevitable. He got up off of the ground, wiped the tears and dirt from His face and went to face His fate. Maybe contrasting Him with the disciples will help you see the power that He derived from accepting the obvious.

You recall that when Jesus went to the Garden to pray, He requested that His disciples get together and pray on His behalf. They had had a busy day. It was late. The physical won over the spiritual, and they fell asleep. Meanwhile, Jesus, who had had an even tougher day, agonized in prayer over the impending battle for the souls of men. When He finally finished praying and accepted what was to come, He calmly awakened the sleeping disciples and prepared them for the mob that was at that very moment making its way through the garden to arrest Him. At that point, the disciples panicked. Peter made a feeble attempt at defending Jesus and then ran with the rest of them to dark corners and back streets of Jerusalem. Throughout the entire trial, flogging, ridicule, and crucifixion, Christ displayed a quiet, determined calm. It was wrapped up in His acceptance of the circumstances and His confidence in the divine plan between Himself and His Father.

The Solution of Serving

There were no more mobs trying to get near enough to touch the edge of His garments. There were no more afternoon sermons on the hills sloping down to the Sea of Galilee. There were no more parades with their palm branches, laughing children, and applauding people. Just a cross-shaped gallows, some nails, a hammer, some disinterested executioners, and the salvation of the human race.

I find it hard to understand, but at the one time in Jesus' earthly ministry when he needed to be concentrating on His own problems, He chose to accommodate the needs of others. In His example we find a key necessity for a rested heart. Jesus knew that rest doesn't come in serving self, but in serving others. He knew that His own pain could never be an excuse for ignoring the pain of others.

He looked down from the cross and saw the middle-aged woman who had, as a teenager, submitted to the God she loved and offered her womb as an incubator for the King of Kings. Mary was graying now. With all that had transpired in the past few days, she looked beaten. He spoke to the one disciple He was sure would be responsible enough to fulfill His request. He asked John to make sure that she was cared for.

Jesus hung between social scum. He was the lily floating in the cesspool. But He knew that He was dying to give hope to the very men with whom He was crucified. One thief mocked Him. The other asked Him for help. Jesus turned his tired and bloody head far enough to catch the man's eyes. He gave Him a promise and a confidence that they would both be in paradise together. That man became the first convert of the crucified Lord. (The last shall be first).

It's hard to understand why men of every culture maintain such a morbid fascination with death. But they do. On that Friday morning when they hammered Jesus to the cross, there was quite a crowd taking it all in. Many of them hurled insults at Him and made jokes about His claims to deity. Along with them were a collection of soldiers who had long since turned cynical toward the issue of meaningful life. For them it was just another execution. Just three more useless criminals. Well, not completely useless. Their shoes and coats were still good. They wouldn't be needing them where they were going. The real nice one, the one taken off of Jesus, supplied an interesting distraction. It was too good to tear apart and divide equally. It was worth gambling over.

While people watched, men laughed, and soldiers gambled, Jesus turned His heart toward heaven and prayed a prayer on their behalf. He said, "Father, forgive them. They haven't a clue of what they've done" (Luke 23:34 paraphrased).

Jesus found rest in accepting the cross and serving others. His example is vital to the suffering heart looking for rest. He said, "If anyone wishes to come after me, let him deny himself, and take up his cross, and follow Me" (Mark 8:34). He knew that we can't necessarily change the behavior of others, but we can control our attitudes. He said, ". . . Love your enemies, and pray for those who persecute you" (Matthew 5:44).

All of this may sound like lame advice if you are in the middle of a suffering situation. "Look to Jesus" comes across like a Band-Aid solution because it doesn't really take away the problem—it just gives us a different way of looking at it.

What we *want* is relief. We want our problem or heartache to just go away. And yet the biblical message of rest is that your relief may come from the power you gain when you accept your suffering. Your relief may come from the strength you develop from serving in spite of it.

Remember, Jesus said, "Take My yoke (suffering) upon you and learn of Me, for I am meek and lowly in heart and you shall *find* rest for your souls."

If you are bewildered, badgered, broken, or battered as you try to make your way along the freeways of life, take a rest. You'll find a quiet calm awaiting you when you accept what you cannot change, and serve the very people who contribute to your pain.

CHAPTER 8

Managing Your Expectations

INDULGE me for a moment. Let's flip on our turn signal and pull off the freeway for a while. There's a winding road up ahead I'd love to show you . . . and a little pink house that means more to me than I can describe.

The map of Pennsylvania is dotted with thousands of names of tiny villages and sleepy boroughs that make up its rural backbone. If you look a tad north of Pittsburgh and just a little east of New Castle, you'll find the word *Eastbrook* printed in the smallest type used by the mapmakers. If you run the speed limit, you can make it from one end of this little village to the other in about thirty seconds. It's the kind of town the "Hee Haw" salute was invented for. For most people, it's little more than a word on a sign that agrees with a dot on a map. But there are a handful of people who call this tiny collection of houses huddled around a bend in the road their home.

Up ahead there—right at the point of the bend. That's the house I mentioned to you. The one that stirs up a lot of special memories for me. It's the home of my grandmother. She and Granddad reared my mother and two uncles from this house. Granddad died while I was fairly young, but Grandma maintained that home as a fortress against the unpredictable elements that come with the passing Pennsylvania seasons—and the unpredictable tensions that come with the passing of time.

When my travels as a conference speaker brought me close to western Pennsylvania, I grabbed as many opportunities as I could to drop in at the little pink house in Eastbrook. Crossing the threshold of her back door was like stepping through some curious time warp. But Grandma's house didn't strike you as a step backward in time as much as a visit to a place where time wasn't an issue.

She didn't divvy out time in appointments. Clocks were used for reminding her that something was in the oven, or that she had twenty minutes to go before "Let's Make A Deal" came on. But clocks were never used to limit her availability to people's needs. Time, for her, was a commodity that she invested in her family and friends.

I wish I could have bottled that special blend of scents that met me as I entered her house. It was a mixture of old with new, fresh with stale, and past with future. But as far I was concerned, in the middle of the hurried schedules that make up my typical day, it was the freshest air in town.

Grandma was satisfied. She never struck me as a lady who felt she had been shortchanged in life. She had lived with both pain and tragedy, and didn't begrudge God for either. Because she lived so much of her life for people, she had learned the joy of contentment.

The ravages of age took away her eyesight a few years ago. It was one personal blow that was hard to accept. But once she did, she simply resumed her role as an investor in people.

I was in the area shortly after she moved to a full care facility. Her house had been sold to friends who remodeled and repainted it. (I can't believe they painted over the pink.) During the renovation, the workers accumulated a pile of lumber and trash outside. I stopped by to see the changes they were making and noticed an interesting reminder of my grandma's life on the pile next to the house.

The item that caught my eye was the instruction booklet which came with her wringer washing machine. It probably sat on the back of a closet shelf for the past thirty-five years. I don't remember when she graduated from the wringer machine to an automatic. It was some time after I had left childhood behind. But I do recall, while still enjoying my carefree years as a child, watching Grandma set up her washing machine on laundry day.

The cycles of a wringer machine weren't regulated by an automatic internal timer, but by how fast your hands could work. The clothes went from soapy water to rinse water to a dry tank. But the transfers from one tank to the other were through the barely parted cylinders that made up the wringer.

Across the top of the wringer was a panic bar. If this type of machine served you on laundry day over a long enough period of time, you usually got an opportunity to see if the panic bar worked.

I remember one sad day when Grandma got her fingers too close to the wringers. Before she knew what had happened the two hungry rollers had pulled her arm in up to the elbow. In the shock and pain of the moment she couldn't think to hit the panic bar. Instead, she reversed the gears and rolled her mangled arm out the way that it had come in.

The consumption oriented society that you and I live in takes us through a wringer of a different sort. It does this in a subtle but deliberate way: It simply keeps us *unsatisfied*. Our own artificially-created expectations wring rest from our hearts. They squeeze out our joy and leave our spirits dry and brittle.

No matter what we have, it isn't enough.

Regardless of the quality, it could always be better. They don't make enlarged "We're Number Three" sponge hands to hold up at football games. We find ourselves so driven to *have* the best and *be* the best that it becomes difficult to relax and appreciate where we are and what we have.

"I CAN'T GET NO SATISFACTION"

Keeping the average family unsatisfied is vital to our economic system. In order to lure me to a particular product, an advertiser must create a dissatisfaction for what I have . . . or a nagging desire for things that I don't need.

Every time I take a shower I stare at a good example of the persuasive power of advertising. My home came equipped with the standard fixture for a shower. It always managed to get me completely wet and adequately clean. But I kept seeing an ad on TV showing people standing under a special shower head that spun the water around and sent it pulsating over their backs. The people on the commercial were always smiling and laughing. I thought about the fixture on my shower. It didn't make me smile or laugh. It didn't make my scalp tingle or relax my neck. It just managed to get me completely wet and adequately clean. I *had* to *have* one of those shower heads that made taking a bath a holiday.

The new shower fixture cost me about five times more than the one I took off. But, my back is worth it, right? I installed this new necessity for happiness about nine years ago. The last time I turned the dial from "Normal" to "Pulsating" was about eight years, eleven months, and three weeks ago. Mainly it has served me as a humble shower. But it does a great job of getting me completely wet and adequately clean.

Truthfully, I'm grateful to live in a free market economy. It's a system that offers the greatest opportunities for developing ideas, accommodating needs, and enjoying prosperity. But every good thing has a potential down side. If the best way to keep me coming back for more is to keep me unsatisfied, I'm going to fight a problem with restlessness. And so is my family.

THE FIFTH NECESSITY:
WE MUST DISCIPLINE OUR DESIRES

I get a kick out of watching parents take their kids through the checkout lines at grocery stores. If it isn't bad enough that they bought more items than they intended to, they are forced to push their children through a narrow stall that has a million things they could live without within the arm's length of a two year old. I couldn't figure why stores created those checkout nightmares until I began noticing how many people actually succumb to the pressure to add to their four-foot grocery tab. Those racks filled with hundreds of toys, trinkets, and candy give even the best parent a literal run for his money. ("Yea though I pass through the valley of the shadow of impulse, I will fear no temper tantrums, because I left my kids at home.")

What I'm addressing is the very essence of restlessness. When we lose control of our expectations, we are guaranteed to be robbed of rest. Yet the culture in which we live makes losing control a foregone conclusion! If I have any hope of enjoying the rest God intends for me, I have to remind myself that I am in a constant struggle with my environment to maintain a sense of satisfaction.

When people fail to discipline their desires, they feel incomplete. A gloomy cloud of inadequacy follows them around. It's difficult to maintain deep relationships with such people— their feelings of inadequacy drain your emotions.

When people fail to discipline their desires, they place unbearable demands on a marriage. Their partner is quick to realize his or her dissatisfaction, and if the partner can't supply all that he or she wants, the partner feels a sense of failure.

When people fail to discipline their desires, they compound stress in their children. An environment where the best is always in the future breeds an attitude that makes the present look cheap.

When people fail to discipline their desires, they accommodate the powers within the world system that desire to control them. A heart that finds it hard to accept its position in life is putty in the hands of the Powers of Darkness.

When God had Moses carve the Ten Commandments in stone, He used the first and last commandments as the supports for the other eight. They were sweeping statements that served as catchalls for the wandering passions of man. If we view these as guidelines for contentment (which they are), we will see why it makes such logical sense to place them in the order in which they appear in the Bible.

The first commandment says . . .

> I am the LORD your God, who brought you out of the land of Egypt, out of the house of slavery. You shall have no other gods before Me (Exodus 20:2-3).

A focused affection on the God who sets men free is the best way to enjoy a life of balanced love. God *is* love. He is the essence of its definition. Since love is one of the fundamental needs of man, it stands to reason that we need to begin by loving the Author of love. As we maintain and strengthen our love for Him, we enable our hearts to see the second priority of our existence on earth—people.

The last commandment says . . .

> You shall not covet your neighbors's house; you shall not covet your neighbor's wife or his male servant

or his female servant or his ox or his donkey or anything that belongs to your neighbor (Exodus 20:17).

Coveting has a lot of nasty synonyms: envy, jealousy, lust, greed. . . . It starts in our hearts as a seed but gets watered and fertilized by the inevitable pressures on our pride.

Your best friend gets a promotion with a significant pay raise—the seed germinates.

The new models for next year roll onto the showroom at the car dealerships—the seed sprouts roots.

You go shopping with your best friend, and she fits beautifully into dresses that are the same size she wore when she got married fifteen years ago. You stare at the size inside the dress you are holding and notice that it's gone up four digits since your wedding day. Ah, the seed of coveting is now starting to show above the surface of your personality.

Coveting is material inebriation. It's an addiction to things that don't last and a craving for things that don't really matter. It forces us to depend on tomorrow to bring us the happiness that today couldn't supply.

Contentment Is an Attitude

I was flying to Canada one autumn to speak at a college. I was on a British carrier that had a lot of Europeans on board. The computer that selected my seat had placed me next to a husband and wife in their mid-fifties. They were a Jewish couple from England who had been vacationing in the United States. Other than smiling and saying hello as I sat down, I had not said anything to them for the first hour and a half of our flight. Instead, I enjoyed being privy to a fascinating conversation between a husband and wife who had been through a lot together. Trust me, it wasn't eavesdropping. They were so entirely caught up in their conversation about family,

business, music, fine wines, and politics it was impossible
to shut them out. I didn't want to anyway. These were
the kind of people you'd choose for companions if you
had to be stuck in a lifeboat for a couple weeks.

Midway through dinner they invited me into their
conversation by utilizing the normal small talk questions.
My questions to them were a lot more probing (minding
other peoples' business is part of my job). I learned about
their business endeavors in England, of their wayward
son, of their personal yearning to die in Israel, and of
how their ability to dream at all was nearly dashed as
children. Both narrowly escaped Hitler's gas chambers.
She lost her parents at Dachau. He wasn't sure where
his parents perished.

I asked them what I thought was an intelligent question.

"Are you happy?"

Neither of them spoke for a second. Then this wise
Jewish gentlemen made a smirking sound and slowly
shook his head as he stared straight in front of him.

"You Americans. The bottom line with you is, 'Are
you happy?' You want to make sure that when all is said
and done, you *feel* a certain way. That requires life to be
fair, generous, and free from hassles. Life has been very
unfair to us. We have made, lost, and made again a fortune
of this world's goods. We've never really known a time
when we didn't have to battle fear and uncertainty. But
we never approached life as if it owed us something. We
have had the opportunity to love and to hope. What
more could we need?"

Wise reprimands should be viewed as gifts. I realized
that this decent man had taken the time and the risk to
be honest. In the process he gave me a gift that I could
enjoy for a lifetime.

It is so easy to fall into the trap of "needing" something emotional or superficial before you'll allow yourself
to find contentment. But I learned (from two people

who should know) that contentment doesn't require a formula, it requires an attitude. They had a gentle and quiet peace in their hearts I envied. They weren't living life for what they could get, but for what they had. And because they didn't demand anything from life, life had a hard time letting them down. They were serious and disciplined stewards of their expectations.

They did not covet what they did not possess.

The "Greener Grass" Syndrome

I'm amazed how often people end up envying the very people who envy them! A pastor sat back in his chair listening to the man seated across from him complain about the cross God had given him to bear. This prominent parishioner was regretting that he had chosen the line of work he was in. He knew he should be grateful. After all, since he had bought the majority position in the company, the stock had split twice. The P and L statements for the last three years had supplied him with excellent Christmas bonuses. He and his wife had enjoyed visits to Europe, the Orient, Australia, and most recently, the Iron Curtain countries.

But he fought a lot of guilt.

He had once pursued the pulpit, but took a side road in seminary that placed him in secular work for good. He went on to outline how much he envied the pastor's knowledge of the Bible and his grasp of theology. He wished that *he* had the time to sit around and read the Scriptures all day. Furthermore . . .

The pastor looked past the man's tailored suit to the window through which he could see the two cars parked outside his study. They were the same color, but that was as far as the comparison could go. As soon as this appointment was over, he'd have to take his aging Pontiac home so that his wife could borrow it to do her chores. The odometer broke at 78,000 miles two years ago. As his counselee rambled on about what a spiritual loser he was, the pastor studied the picture framed on the corner of his desk. His two children smiled so broadly and so proudly. They were too young to be self-conscious. But in a few years they'd realize what he already knew. Their teeth needed elaborate orthodontic work. But it wasn't going to happen on his paycheck. He kept thinking of all the times that businessmen had said to him, "Pastor, with your skills, you could have knocked 'em dead in the business arena." They never knew that money was one of the biggest temptations of his life.

Changing places wouldn't solve either one of these men's problems. One man was an ungrateful steward of much, the other was an ungrateful steward of many.

The more we measure our significance by other people's accomplishments, the less we'll be able to feel at rest in our daily lives. A rushed lifestyle is only going to bring more successful people to envy, more unaffordable conveniences to covet, and more failures to regret.

ATTITUDES THAT HINDER

There are certain attitudes that predispose a person to envy. Envy is guaranteed to bring unhappiness. But because no man is an island, an unsatisfied attitude will also take its toll on people close to you. A marriage can find itself paralyzed by discontent. Love can be put to tests that love is not mature enough to pass. And our children can learn the pattern early enough to punish us with an ungrateful spirit throughout their stay under our influence.

We can teach ourselves to be satisfied just as certainly as we can teach ourselves to be unsatisfied. If certain attitudes predispose us to envy, then we need to run an inventory on those attitudes in order to move them toward satisfaction. It's a way to monitor our heart, and to force it back on target.

One way to check your satisfaction quota is to see

how you complete a couple of sentences. The second half of these statements can tell all. Let me help by completing them several ways. I may not hit the areas that you struggle in, but the ones I do offer should give you an idea of how to personalize them.

If only I had . . .
    a job
    a better job
    a more understanding boss
    enough money to retire on
    a bigger house
    a thinner waist
    a better education
    a husband
    a different husband
    a child
    a lifestyle like . . .
    taken more time out for my family
If only I hadn't . . .
    dropped out of school
    been forced to get married
    had an abortion
    started drinking
    run over that child
    been fired
    run up so many debts
    trusted that smooth-talking con artist
    neglected my wife
    quit that job
    sold that stock
    bought that stock
If only they had . . .
    given me more playing time
    recognized my potential
    offered me the job
    encouraged me to apply myself in school
    supported me in my sports
    been honest with me
    stuck with me

If only they hadn't . . .
  abandoned me as a baby
  discouraged me
  prejudged me
  pushed me so hard to achieve
  lied to me
  been so interested in making money
  been ashamed of my handicap

If only . . . if only . . . if only. The starting words for unfulfilled expectations or nagging regrets. No one is immune to their destructive impact. Because we are people and not machines, we can't deny the impact of our past mistakes or disappointments. Nor can we turn deaf ears or blind eyes to the many desires of this world that may be out of reach.

Dealing with a Disappointing Past

Too many people are unsatisfied with where they are because they don't like the path they took to get there. Often the path to the present was not of their personal choosing.

Most people have had to deal with the pain that comes when they don't meet other people's expectations. But all rejection is not equal. The pain of being rejected by a parent or spouse is far more devastating than being rejected for our ideas or unappreciated for our contributions. Some people can't seem to move out of neutral in the present because their primary "reason for living" let them down in the past.

Others put their life in gear but take off in the wrong direction. A disappointing past can throw our expectations out of whack. We suddenly view acquisitions or status as an antidote for the pain of our past. We think that success will prove we can amount to something, that marriage will prove we are worth loving, that wealth will get people's attention.

I remember an enlightening conversation with a plastic surgeon. Much of what he did brought a healthy transformation to his patients. A rebuilt nose could bring an end to years of teasing. A restructured jaw could restore what the disfigurement of an accident had stolen.

"But you know, Tim," he confided, "many people come into my office for a new look, when what they really want is a new *life*."

A key, then, to experiencing lasting rest in our lives is refusing to allow past disappointments to cause us to pursue unhealthy desires. We need to be disciplined at keeping our past hurts in perspective.

I'm so grateful that we don't have to do this alone. The message of the Bible is that God wants to comfort us in our sorrows, fill our voids, and forgive our sins. There is no purchase that will remove the hurt of rejection. There is no activity that will cover the consequences of our negligence. Emptiness and pain need the permanent presence of a God who promises to never leave us or let us down. When our past is handled in a healthy way, we have a better chance of having healthy expectations.

Is It Okay to Dream?

Of course, there is a healthy desire within most of us to improve ourselves and our positions. It is an instinctive quality placed within us by God. To deny it would be foolish, and to ignore it would be sacrilegious.

Certain additions to our lives are capable of giving us a lot of joy. A bigger house could give some badly needed relief from the cramped quarters you presently endure. A graduate degree could offer you a better platform from which to serve people and a better income through which you could accommodate your family needs. An exotic vacation could allow you to make many beautiful memories with people you love. A spouse could give you an opportunity to love and be loved. There's nothing wrong with these desires.

But if we are going to dream, we need to make sure that we are doing two things at the same time.

First, *we need to make sure that we are pursuing legitimate goals*. What is a legitimate goal? Anything that improves your ability to love and serve God and people is a legitimate goal. Is there room, then, for acquiring things that accommodate you? Sure. Beautiful possessions have a legitimate place in a balanced person's life. Possessions can never "complete" you, but they can be rewards that come from hard work and conscientious living. They adorn our life—but don't make our life. To *pursue* possessions in order to fill a void is folly. And if in the process of pursuing them we neglect God-given responsibilities, then they are double trouble. Instead of being rewards they become treacherous obstacles to healthy living.

If you could have joined me on a visit to a particular lady I'm thinking about, you would know exactly what I mean. I met Marilyn and her family the way a lot of ministers meet people for the first time—through their pain. She and her husband nearly lost their son through a terrible accident. The boy had been thrown from his dirt bike while racing through the desert. It only took a split second for the little boy's body to be mangled, and a family's heart to be broken. Most families would have come apart under the weight and pain this accident brought, but Marilyn's resolve and God's grace made the difference. She refused to accept defeat. She prayed that boy out of a coma, out of bed, out of a wheelchair, and finally, out of crutches. It was a tribute to her love and persistence.

Several years after the accident I stopped by Marilyn's home to visit her and her son. I drove up to a nice house in a nice community. The inside of the home was even nicer. It was comfortably furnished, tastefully decorated, and extremely roomy. After chatting in the family room for a while, we all moved into the kitchen so that she could fix us a soft drink.

I couldn't help notice her refrigerator door. It was covered with pictures of houses, sleek yachts, exotic places, and piles of money. Naturally I inquired about them. She was happy to tell me all about it.

After her son had recovered from the worst of his injuries, she and her husband decided to make a career move. The company that hired them dangled promises of riches beyond the average person's imagination. They worked day and night to build their profile in the company. They regularly attended sales meetings at their office where articulate company leaders made them feel inadequate. They were reminded that where they were was inferior to where they could be. They were told to dream without limits, to visualize themselves enjoying the very best that life could offer. Their boss encouraged them to put pictures on their refrigerator and bathroom mirror of the things they thought would bring them a lot of joy. They were told not to accept "mediocrity and second best," but to go for the top.

I looked around her house. It seemed so warm and comfortable. Definitely upper middle class.

Then I looked at the boy.

I thought of Jesus raising Jairus's daughter from the dead. Although He had not worked in an instant way with this lady's son, his recovery was no less a miracle. Her boy was supposed to be dead, but he was very much alive. Doctors said that if he did live, he'd be a vegetable. Instead, he was mentally alert. They said that if he did come out of the coma, he would probably never walk again. He proved them wrong once more by starring on his school's track team.

She walked me to my car. When the boy was out of earshot, I voiced my concern about the shift in her preoccupations. She had been given a healthy chunk of earth's material pleasures, but even more importantly . . . she had her son back from the dead. Why was she so obsessed with getting more? She tried to defend herself. Wealth, she said, would give her a greater "platform" from which to tell the story of her son. Wealth would help her influence people for Christ. The resources could be used to finance the message.

I closed the car door and rolled down the window. I wanted to be honest with her, but the words came slow and hard.

"Marilyn . . . you're trying so hard to rationalize wrong priorities. If the only way you can gain an audience's respect is by outshining them materially, you're doomed to have fickle friends all your life."

If the only way to get someone to listen to her was to shout from the deck of her yacht or over the whine of her private jet, she was in trouble. The truth was that she wasn't satisfied with what she had . . . and never would be.

She and her husband pursued the wrong dreams. Ultimately, their marriage blew apart and their second child ended up in court on drug charges. They pursued legitimate things for illegitimate reasons. Instead of letting them become rewards of conscientious work, they became obsessions of an unsatisfied and restless heart.

Don't be snookered by "The Lifestyles of the Rich and Famous." Material acquisition cannot fill the void within our lives. Status and influence cannot substitute for our need to love and be loved. You want proof? Trace the trail of broken marriages and troubled children that plague many of the people showcased on that television show.

No, there is nothing wrong with living comfortably, dressing well, driving a nice car, or being famous. These are legitimate rewards that always have responsibilities attached to them. But when they become the things that motivate us, complete us, or sustain us, we're sure to wake up one morning and find ourselves empty. Hollow to the core.

Billy Graham put it well when he said that the smallest package he ever saw was a man wrapped up wholly in himself. Undisciplined desires can make small packages out of big people. Jesus said, "Seek first His kingdom and His righteousness; and all these things (the necessities that sustain and satisfy) shall be added to you" (Matthew 6:33).

BRINGING CONTENTMENT ON BOARD

Remember that I said we need to be doing two things in order to maintain disciplined desires? The first thing is to make sure that we are pursuing legitimate goals. The second thing is to *make sure that we are making the most of where we are.* You know what I mean. You've seen people who are so busy stretching for the brass ring that they forget to enjoy the merry-go-ride.

We need to make Contentment a member of our internal board of directors. Give him the freedom to ask the hard questions when you start feeling you need something more to bring you happiness. If you do, be prepared to mumble a lot to yourself. He likes to ask questions like:

Can you afford this?

Do you have to give up much of the few spare hours that you have left to take advantage of this thing?

Will this free you up to spend the time necessary to maintain your commitments to family and friends?

Will this in any way frustrate your relationship with God?

Do you see why people don't want Contentment in the boardroom of their hearts? He demands that we place proper value on the things that bring us joy.

An unsatisfied heart in a life with much blessing is sin. As long as we allow this constant craving to dominate our hearts we will be denied inner rest. As Calvin Miller wrote:

> The world is poor because her fortune is buried in the sky and all her treasure maps are of the earth.[10]

The only way we can keep our expectations and desires disciplined is with God's help. A relationship with God that is personal yields a set of desires that are practical. Knowing that He loves us and has forgiven us keeps us from wanting the wrong things. By following His example when He walked the earth, we develop priorities that sustain our heart both now and through the future.

CHAPTER 9

Managing Your Strengths

AUTHOR John Trent tells of an eye-opening incident on his first day in graduate school.

He had enrolled at Dallas Seminary with good intentions, but since he had arrived there he seriously wondered if he would make it. He walked into his first class with legitimate apprehensions. After all, this wasn't "party time" college any more. This was an environment where professors rolled fifty-dollar theological words off of their tongues.

The dean had made it clear in orientation that Dallas wouldn't spoon-feed anyone. You either kept up the work load, or you would find yourself in an unrecoverable position.

The assistant had just passed out the syllabus for the class, and after reading it John mentally calculated that he was already three weeks behind.

The professor walked up to the lectern and stared around the room at the sea of faces. John felt that he could read the wise man's mind: *So this is the leadership of tomorrow's church. We're in trouble!* Despite this unnerving scrutiny, everything John had heard about this man underscored that he was a loving and caring gentleman. Dr. Howard Hendricks was one of the main reasons he had enrolled at Dallas.

The very first words out of the professor's mouth sent ice water through John's veins.

"Gentlemen, I am going to give you the most significant test you will ever have during your studies here at Dallas Seminary."

John groaned silently. *So much for all the nice things that I heard about this guy.*

"How you do on this test will determine how you do in the ministry."

Great, I'm getting cut from the team before I even get a chance to play.

"Those who do well invariably succeed. Those who flunk this test invariably struggle and falter in ministry."

You're not wasting any time separating the sheep from the goats, are you, prof? I knew I should've had more theological training before I came here. He's going to split some theological hair and make me look like a jerk.

"On the three-by-five card in front of you I want you to list your three greatest weaknesses."

That's it? That's all? Piece of cake! If being a success just takes a working knowledge of my inadequacies, then I'm gonna be one of the greatest ministers the church has ever had.

John joined his fellow seminarians in writing down their weaknesses. They all wrote quickly. The only problem any of them seemed to have was deciding *which* of their many weaknesses would be considered the top three. He finished writing, laid down his pen, and stared up at the professor with a look of confidence on his face.

Dr. Hendricks continued. "Now, gentlemen, turn over your card and answer this second question."

I knew it was too good to be true! Here comes the zinger. I'm doomed. Maybe it's not too late to get back some of my matriculation fee . . . .

"What are your three greatest *strengths*?"

John joined his colleagues in experiencing temporary paralysis in his writing hand. Men weren't rushing
to fill out their card. Some simply stared at it. Others
tapped the tip of their nose with their pen, or frowned
intently at the wall as though they hoped to find the
answer written on it.

Answering that question seemed—well, contradic-
tory to John's calling. He was supposed to be a humble
man of the cloth. Listing his greatest strengths seemed
like cheap boasting. Wasn't there something in the Bible
about God giving grace to the humble and opposition
to the proud? (James 4:6) Zeroing in on what made him
strong and even superior to his fellow man was discom-
forting. Besides, God gets a lot of mileage out of working
through men's weaknesses. Didn't He say to Paul, "My
grace is sufficient for you, for [my] power is perfected in
weakness"? (2 Corinthians 12:9).

Across the room from John another young man sat
struggling with the same question. Fifteen years later, I
still struggle with it.

Dr. Hendricks was right. Knowledge of our personal
strengths is critical to a calm and ordered life.

It's easy enough to list weaknesses. All of us have
had plenty of help on that score. Parents, teachers,
coaches, friends, and enemies made sure we didn't overlook a single one.

It has been my observation that most people grow
up with lots of negative reinforcement. Our culture occasionally rewards but seldom remembers those who come
in second. The list of those who "also ran" doesn't get
much space in the yearbook. "Close" only counts in horse-
shoes and nuclear war.

It's certainly no problem to concentrate on our failures and weaknesses. We can be ready to conduct a
guided tour through our inadequacies at a moment's
notice.

But the fact remains that you and I *do* have
strengths. God-given resources worth developing and

managing. And if we want to cope with the incredible pressures of our hurried world, we need to isolate those strengths and put them to work.

It's a matter of stewardship.

THE SIXTH NECESSITY:
WE MUST MANAGE OUR RESOURCES

The word *stewardship* isn't used as much as it used to be. But it's an excellent word for our discussion. It refers to the *conscientious management of the things that really matter.* It requires responsibility and maturity. Stewardship demands work and doesn't accept excuses. It forces people to reevaluate priorities. It makes them reconsider their purposes for living.

When I meet older people advising me to slow down, spend more time with people, and develop my talents, I hear wise experience talking. They have learned through waste and regret what God would rather teach us through principles of stewardship. They have learned that resources are to be conserved and invested, not ignored or squandered.

Although I can't speak from the wisdom of years, I can speak from the platform of observation. Most of the unhappy people who approach me for counsel suffer from a simple syndrome: They are poor stewards of their lives. They have developed a bad habit of ignoring the important and prioritizing the nonessential.

There is only one way out of this dilemma, and few are willing to take it. The path to relief is painful. It requires reordering their priorities—deliberately changing the inner price tags all of us attach to the elements of our lives. For some people, that is just too much. They would rather accept the discomfort and slow death of emotional cancer than endure the surgery that could save them.

It's too bad, because this sixth key for genuine rest could give them the platform and the discipline to maintain the other five.

When Dr. Hendricks challenged that seminary class to isolate and articulate their greatest strengths, he was not asking them to be boastful, haughty, or proud. He was calling them to be realistic, honest, and conscientious. He knew that life becomes a threat when we are taking from it but not giving back. He knew that we become a drain on people if we *use* relationships rather than *contribute* to them. He knew that our greatest joy would be found in investing our gifts rather than burying them.

His kind of thinking comes from the presupposition that every man and woman is born rich. We may come into the world in our birthday suit and leave in our burial suit, but our greatest treasures are wrapped up in the things that can't be kept in a safety deposit box. We are born with intrinsic value—the very desire of God's heart.

He would not sacrifice His Son for someone who has no value.

He would not give eternal life to someone who has no value.

It might help us, as we develop this discussion on managing our gifts, to divide our true assets into three categories: CALLING, CONVICTIONS, and CAPABILITIES. These groupings can serve as a checklist as we determine what kind of a steward we are.

STEWARDING OUR CALLING

Part of the frustration of the hurried life is that it has a way of trivializing our commitments. We have certain callings in life that must be maintained, but life hassles us into giving these callings a second-class status. I'm not referring to "calling" in a mystical sense. I don't know anything about that kind of stuff. But I do know there are certain responsibilities we are either given or choose to accept which cannot be ignored.

Vocational callings

Think of my calling as a minister, for example. I may work under the wing of an independent ministry, and I may speak at different churches Sunday by Sunday, but I am, nonetheless, a minister. If you were to visit my office you would notice the framed diplomas and the ordination certificate that serve as visible credentials to my calling. I have a close friend who has debated with me at length how I knew that I was "called" to the ministry. Although I have done a poor job of explaining to him how I knew that I was supposed to be a minister, we both agree this is what I'm supposed to be doing.

Because of my calling there are certain responsibilities I must maintain. My freedoms are limited. People's expectations are high. Because of my role as teacher, helper, and advisor, my calling requires me to be a *learner*. I can't coast. I can't fake it. I can't drop pearls of wisdom from a small window in an ivory tower. The people I serve deserve messages wrung from the crucible of my daily experience and walk with God. The people who look to me for direction need to know that my advice is more than theory or regurgitation of seminary textbooks. If I'm going to prepare them for daily battle, I have to smell the gunpowder and know my way around the trenches.

My calling restricts me, but it is in submission to those restrictions that I become the most valuable to people. It goes with the territory of serving. There are many professions that call for serious commitments—and restrictions—from those who work within them. Doctors, teachers, managers, researchers, public servants, and attorneys all work in fields which call for a high level of commitment. We must steward our profession well. If someone has either chosen or accepted a position as role model to young people, for example, they have forfeited certain rights. That's why sports figures need to think twice before they exercise their independence in areas that could mislead children. Jesus said that people who lead children astray will not do so without consequences. (Actually, His language is a lot stronger than that. Read it for yourself in Matthew 18:1-10.)

When we are good stewards of our calling we counter the pressures of a hurried lifestyle. Hurried lifestyles push us to take shortcuts. Too many of them cost us in the areas of honesty and self-esteem. When we feel that we are cheating those for whom or with whom we are called to work, something within us breaks down. We can't expect to defraud ourselves and still feel calm inside.

Relational callings

On August 19, 1972, I stood before a group of witnesses and said that I would devote my life to Darcy Dirks. I was not drugged, drunk, or hallucinating when I said it. The two witnesses who signed our marriage license will testify to that. Since then, there have been opportunities to go back on my word. Furthermore, my wife and I have given each other reasons to wish we hadn't been so quick to agree to the vows.

Nevertheless, the vows were exchanged. The contract was signed. It became one of my callings in life—a calling that God takes very seriously. The more seriously I take my calling as a husband the better off my marriage is.

On three occasions my wife went to the hospital to give birth to three children who have a lot of my physical characteristics. The moment they were conceived they became part of my calling. As a steward of my calling to fatherhood, I cannot hope to come close to meeting their needs without a deliberate and individual devotion to each one of them.

This is when our high-speed world really puts on the pressure. Being an effective father and being a "success" at the same time is sometimes impossible. When it comes to choices in this area, the lure of the fast lane increases its pull. Kids just don't cooperate as well as the laws of money. Kids don't reward our egos as much as the shiny steps at the top of the ladder of success. That's why the sixth key to rest carries so much clout. It's the acid test of our priorities. If we are good stewards of our callings we will consistently refuse to sacrifice the permanent on the altar of the immediate. We will place our callings in divine order. Regardless of how noble our vocation and how many people directly benefit from our involvement in it, God would not condone the forsaking of primary callings (marriage and children) for secondary callings (work).

STEWARDING OUR CONVICTIONS

Some people paint themselves into a restless corner by failing to maintain their convictions. We've already considered the sad outcome of those who refuse to "live within the limits" in an earlier chapter.

Convictions represent an incredible source of strength. Maybe you've never seen them in that light before. Maybe you've never included them in an inventory of your personal resources. And yet your personal convictions must be counted among your most precious possessions. The pressures to conform, to ignore, to excuse, or to surrender bombard us every day. If I want to maintain a calm heart in the midst of a hectic and fast-paced culture, I must be careful to keep my convictions uncompromised.

Convictions are an asset to our spirit and a resource to our relationships. They function as the cement within our love . . . the strength within our purpose . . . the resolve within our hope. And they must be guarded with a passion. Without consistent convictions, an individual finds himself at the mercy of life's shifting winds. (A good passage of scripture on this subject is James 1:6-8).

Too many people think that ethics can be determined by the situation. Yet making the rules as you go along is certain to produce conflict both inside and outside of your heart. Feelings get hurt. Lives get damaged beyond repair. That's why we can't afford to ignore the impact of convictions.

Please note, however, that convictions have nothing to do with the "collective conscience" of our society. The collective conscience is no more qualified to determine truth than the individual. Sometimes the collective conscience is little more than the pooling of ignorance. If the majority is to be our standard, we're in serious trouble. Charles Colson reminds us to "Never confuse the will of the majority with the will of God." If we want to steward convictions, we must turn to God.

That's why a steady diet of Bible reading and Bible study is so crucial to the well-managed life. Its pages contain universal truths we can rely on when we aren't sure of what to do. In my work, I run into all kinds of people. Those who make it through life with the least amount of conflicts from their personal choices are those who submit to a clear set of convictions. And those who submit to convictions invariably maintain a consistent intake of God's word. I'm not legalistic about when or how often a person must read the Scriptures. I just know that those who come to the Bible on a habitual basis to gain direction for living make better choices.

Stewarding our convictions helps us when our children throw us the curves for which they are justly famous. We are enabled to make the difficult choices effective parenting demands.

Stewarding our convictions can keep us *out* of the wrong kind of trouble, but *in* the right kind of trouble. When our convictions are worth fighting for, we become an invaluable asset to our culture. People who are willing to lay their popularity and status on the line for the underdogs, victims, and legitimate causes of life insure there will be a tomorrow worth fighting for.

In a restless world where rules are relative and people vacillate from one urgency to the next, convictions will set you free. They will support you when you are alone, defend you when you are attacked, and exonerate you when you are falsely accused. They may be the only friend you have at certain dark moments of your life. But if you steward them well, they can give you a solid reputation, a secure marriage, confident kids, insured work. . . and maybe even save your life.

Those who love the truth will live by it. Those who live by it will enjoy a complete and balanced life. The Bible promises peace and rest to the individual who stewards his convictions. (Psalm 1 is a good place to start.)

Maintaining our callings and managing our convictions will enable us to steward the third major treasure of our life.

STEWARDING OUR CAPABILITIES

Every person has talent. When talents are harnessed and disciplined they become skills. When skills are used, power is unleashed. When power is used to contribute to a legitimate purpose, people benefit. Individuals who steward their personal capabilities make their life, with its talents, part of the cultural solution to frustration and confusion.

But too many people run into problems because stewarding our capabilities is hard. It means denying oneself, sacrificing, and failing in order to perfect what we are gifted at doing. From early childhood we can pick up the patterns that either reward us for our efforts or punish us for our negligence. The one pattern that seems to dominate the lives of teenagers I work with is their difficulty in delaying gratification. It might be in the area of their studies, sports, a job, or sex. Regardless, the outcome is the same. Their inability to discipline themselves and channel their talents and skills in proper directions brings them an inner restlessness that shows. They are angry, frustrated, and doomed to suffer throughout their life until they become willing to submit their strengths to discipline.

Well-managed talents, on the other hand, give a

person a strong sense of purpose and value. They help us to counter the overwhelming pressure from culture to make us feel insecure. Insecure people are never static with their insecurity. Invariably they impose their insecurities on the people around them. Most insecurities are difficult to overlook; they are deep-seated and complex. But one remedy is developing the ability to harness your capabilities, and use them in a positive way.

Every Christian has spiritual gifts. These were given by God in order to round out the church. Attending church Sunday after Sunday without serving is poor stewardship of our capabilities. God can bring us a depth of joy and stability when we are carefully guarding and using the talents and gifts He gave us.

Of course every dimension of our life requires balance and boundaries. Talents are our personal strengths. But poorly maintained talents can become overtaxed. In many peoples' lives, their weaknesses are nothing more than strengths pushed to the limit. If we push our spiritual gifts to an extreme we burn out. If we push our emotional gifts to an extreme we get depressed. If we push our physical gifts to an extreme we get sick.

Probably the biggest battle most of us fight is in the stewarding of our time. It's the one gift in our life that was given to us in a fixed amount. Each time we use it, it is forever spent. That's why we should be careful to invest generous chunks of it in things and people that have eternal significance. Don't fall into the trap of thinking that only those who wear the cleric's collar or the nun's habit have the opportunity to invest in forever. The little eyes that peek at you through the rails of a crib, or the spouse who sleeps inches from you every night can make your gift of time an investment in eternity.

WHEN STEWARDSHIP COMES HOME

I mentioned earlier in the book that my mother died of cancer. From the time the doctors discovered it to the time it took her life was only five months. Her decline was swift and unstoppable. Surgery, radiation, and chemotherapy had no effect on it.

Mom had been a serious steward of the things that mattered. She never forsook her calling as a wife and mother. She didn't require an opinion poll to determine which way she should lean in a conflict. Her convictions served her just fine. And she isolated her talents as a servant early in her married life. She gave to her family and friends from a generous heart.

A few weeks before her allotted gift of time was up she was hanging onto this life by an invisible thread and the many visible tubes and gadgets around her bed. The intensive care unit of the Greenville Hospital in Greenville, Pennsylvania is a circular room. The beds surround a central hub where the nurses monitor the vital signs that come from the various patients' equipment. The only thing that gives privacy to a patient is a curtain that can be pulled around the bed. There is one exception, though—a single room built into the circle for extremely ill patients.

That's where Mom lay dying.

My younger brother who lives in the Phoenix area and I had flown back to see her three times in the five months that she was sick. During the last month I called every morning to see how she made it through the night, and every night to see how she made it through the day. My father stayed with her every day. My three other brothers and sister all lived in the area. They stopped by regularly, almost daily, to be with her.

Shortly before Mom died, a wealthy, influential member of that small Pennsylvania community was admitted to the intensive care unit for observation. On the third night of his stay in the hospital, he had a discussion with the nurse who was preparing him to go to sleep for the night. I called the unit shortly after she finished working with him. She couldn't help but relate their conversation.

This young nurse was a Christian. She knew of our family's love for Christ and of my mother's quiet but compelling testimony. She told me that the man she talked with was one of the most powerful men in the community. He wielded great influence, even at the hospital. Yet he had lain in that hospital room for three days without a single visitor. He had a wife, and he had children, but they had not come by.

As she was giving him his medicine he inquired of the patient in the private room.

"Oh, that's Mrs. Kimmel," the nurse replied.

He wanted to know about my father and my brothers and sister. She told him all about them and mentioned that her two sons in Phoenix had been back to see her several times and called daily to check on her status.

He asked about Mom's condition.

"Mrs. Kimmel will die any day," the nurse told him. "If she lives a week, we'll all be surprised."

At that point this man of influence dropped his head back on his pillow and got quiet. Just before she walked away he looked up at her with tears in his eyes.

"You know," he said in a husky voice, "I would gladly trade places with Mrs. Kimmel and die a week from now, if for that week I could have a spouse and children who care enough about me not to make me die alone."

The words of Eleanor Roosevelt ring true:

> One's philosophy is not best expressed in words. It is expressed in the choices one makes. In the long run, we shape our lives and we shape ourselves. The process never ends until we die. And the choices we make are ultimately our responsibility.[11]

Stewardship . . .
the conscientious management
of the things that really matter.

CHAPTER 10

Bringing Rest to Your Marriage

M Y wife and I derive a great deal of joy from exploring the dusty and cluttered back rooms of antique stores. We have a way of sniffing out the best ones in town. To us, they are a collage of history and a market of memories. When you live in an age where today is going to be obsolete tomorrow, it's nice to visit an era where days lingered for decades. People weren't in that big of a hurry to see what was around the next corner in life. They were satisfied to enjoy where they were.

Because I'm usually ready to join my generation in a race to see what's around the next corner, these visits to antique stores serve as a mental therapy for me. If the retailers of history aren't outrageous in their pricing, I occasionally bring some of these memories home with me.

There is one item I passed up in a store not long ago. I wish now I would have purchased it.

One rainy afternoon in central California, I explored an antique shop that was more like the personal museum of a single family. The proprietor must have purchased the entire estate of this family to establish his business. Many of the items bore the monograms or names of the movers and shakers of this home. They must have enjoyed their zenith years between the 1880s to the 1920s. One item from the collection made a touching but sad statement about the couple who sat at the apex of this family tree. It was their wedding album.

You've probably seen one of these victorian albums. The brocade cloth stretching over the padded outer cover was faded from age. The dozen leaves inside were originally edged in gold. A century's worth of handling, however, had rubbed away all but a trace of it. Only three pictures remained of the original collection.

In the first, the bride and groom had posed for their formal portrait. They were both sitting in straightback chairs with blank expressions on their faces. There was about a foot of empty space between the two chairs. The new couple weren't touching each other.

The second picture was the solo portrait of the new bride. She was probably in her late teens. Her eyes carried a look of caution and fear. They betrayed the anxiety that she no doubt felt about the approaching first night of her honeymoon, but they also seemed to reflect a concern for the mysteries that lay ahead in the life that she and her new husband would live. These first two pictures were the traditional poses I've seen in many of these old albums.

The next few leaves were missing the photos that normally carried images of in-laws and siblings. The last leaf took me by surprise. It was a break from tradition—a picture you would expect to see in a modern wedding album, but would assume out of place and out of character for a wedding album assembled over a hundred years ago. The fading photograph captured a peak at the celebration and the joy that must have made up this wedding reception so long ago. The groom was standing with one arm wrapped around the waist of his new bride and the other holding a champagne glass high above his head. The bride had replaced her sober portrait look for a full-toothed laugh. Surrounding them were half a dozen friends who had raised their glasses to toast their future.

I was sitting in a rocking chair that had been part of this couple's collection since early in their marriage. They had probably rocked their children through infancy and a few thunderstorms in this chair. If it could talk, it could probably tell a lot of anecdotes about the girl behind the laugh and the man who held her close. It watched this laughing young bride with sparkling eyes and shiny hair grow gray an old. It helped this anxious groom through a few sleepless nights.

Now all of the earthly memories of this couple were collecting dust in the corner of an antique shop at the end of a road in California.

One thought kept occupying my mind as I stared at the picture of these newlyweds. They were now dead. The physical remains of these two people who once lived and loved were probably lying side by side in some overgrown cemetery. Their wedding album and their possessions apparently didn't carry much value to the new generations they ultimately sired.

But fading on the back leaf of the album was evidence they once married, and they once laughed.

From the look of the quality of their furniture, they must have done all right. From the look of the stamps on their trunk, and the curios collected during their travels around the world, they must have enjoyed years of adventure. From the look of everything, this couple who laughed at their wedding must have done a lot of laughing during their walk through time together. Although they were dead, in my mind part of them was very much alive.

A couple weeks after I visited the antique store I was driving down a street not far from my home. I had my daughter with me, and she was carefully fulfilling her role as "garage sale look-out." She watched for the signs nailed to telephone poles or taped to boxes that give directions to some front yard flea market.

"There's one, Daddy!"

I slowed down to read it.

Garage Sale
GETTING DIVORCED
Everything Must Go

We followed the signs to the house, parked the car, and walked up the driveway. The various items for sale had been placed in neat rows on each side of the driveway with a four-foot aisle separating them. The gal operating the sale had taken a piece of chalk and written a revealing message on the concrete aisle: *HIS STUFF* (with an arrow pointing left) and *MY STUFF* (with an arrow pointing to the right).

Just about everything a young couple would need to start up housekeeping was there: dishes, linens, cookware, stemware—even a washer and dryer. Sitting on the middle of a card table on the right side of the driveway was an eight-by-ten-inch gold frame holding a wedding picture of the young couple.

They, too, had laughed.

The young girl running the sale didn't look as if she had changed much in the few years since the picture was taken . . . except for the laugh. It had been replaced by a seasoned look of contempt. She told me to make her an offer for the frame; she was in a mood to bargain. I asked if she wanted the picture. She gave me a cynical look and said she'd throw it in at no extra charge. I decided this was one picture frame that I could live without.

That laughing couple in the eight-by-ten-inch frame was very much alive, but their marriage was dead. The young couple with whom I shared a memory in an antique store one rainy afternoon was dead, but their marriage had been full of life.

What Makes the Difference?

What causes two marriages to start out with the same intentions, but end in such different ways? Since I didn't know either couple personally, I can't really answer those questions for them. Nevertheless, the end of one couple illustrates a universal truth, and the end of the other illustrates a universal dilemma.

Most of us who are married laughed in front of the cameraman at our wedding. We probably laughed for the few days that followed it, too. But the frustrations and pressures that begin stalking a new couple at the wedding altar don't take long before they make their presence known. The ability to maintain a marriage commitment becomes a challenge—a challenge this hurried half of the twentieth century doesn't give us much help with. Our culture punishes those who attempt to endure. When the battle of the bedroom gets too intense, it makes throwing in the monogrammed towel as easy as possible.

We all know divorce is bad news. Those who have endured it would be the first to share how painful and emptying the break-up of a love partnership can be. The new generation reaching marriageable age fights the inclination to become disillusioned. They want to believe it can work, but it's so difficult to find adequate role models.

That's because married couples are forced to row against a strong and contrary current of culture. They find the love that brought them to the altar threatened by the distractions of their struggles and the demands of their successes. They find that the biggest challenge of having a dog, a station wagon, and 3.2 kids is keeping the whole group together long enough to steal a little happiness.

Not all marriages are hurting, but it's hard to find one that isn't hassled. Hurried living does that to you. The most conscientious couple can find their commitment tested just because they have too many legitimate responsibilities competing for the time it takes to maintain a healthy marriage.

The average couple is deluged with more information than it knows how to interpret or assimilate. But if they want to stay competitive in a world that waits for no one, they have to try. Information demands choices, work arenas demand action, children demand attention, and the marriage gets whatever energy remains.

Only a few couples come to this rat race with a clue of what they are up against. The parents who reared their children in the 1950s and 1960s could never have anticipated the extent of the pressure that would greet their children when they walked down the aisle. It's easy to see why so many couples have a difficult time coping. Their best intentions are up against a lot of competition. That probably explains why some couples counter with extreme measures they hope will bring solutions.

I meet a lot of these types of people in my travels—those who have shot their television, moved to the mountains, and are educating their children themselves. I both admire and respect their decisions. Some of them are doing an excellent job of combating the destructive pressures on their marriage and children.

But most couples simply cannot afford the luxury of isolation. To suggest, as some do, that this sort of withdrawal is a realistic plan for the masses falls far short of practical reasoning. Furthermore, isolation assumes that the problem is environmental. There's no question that our contaminated culture pounds its pressures home every day that we are exposed to it. But the biggest determining factor for a successful marriage is not the environment in which the marriage functions, but the *attitude* within the heart of the couple.

Most marriages are going to have to learn how to win the battle against their culture by facing it head-on. Pressures won't diminish in the future. We're all guaranteed that the battle for our commitments will increase. Since most couples are going to live in the mainstream of life, we need a strategy for them. There are specific actions a couple can take to bring a little sanity back into the middle of the rat race (there are 101 suggestions in the appendix), but in this chapter I want to concentrate on the *attitudes* behind the action. I'm convinced that the biggest part of the battle for our love is fought between our ears. It can be complicated by the pressures outside of us, but if the attitudes and conditions within our hearts aren't right, our marriage is doomed regardless of outside forces.

In other words, successful marriages do not require certain conditions in order to be successful. Some of the greatest marriages in history were maintained under the worst conditions. War, imprisonment, separation, famine, poverty, and sickness do not stop committed people from maintaining their commitment. They are merely the factors that must be dealt with as two people who love each other face their world together.

That's the good news for hurried marriages. The necessities for a secure relationship are not dependent on life treating us a certain way. We don't have to assume that the tensions of hurried living will get the best of us. In fact, we can approach the mysteries that lie in the future with complete calm—and I'll even take it a step beyond that. We can actually *look forward* to the complications and competition that will face married couples in the future.

To do this, however, we will need a perception of what love is, an understanding of what love requires, and a commitment to carry out those requirements. We all know this is easier to discuss than to implement. Love is always easier to deal with in an abstract way. When it comes down to living out our perceptions of love, we can run into problems. That's why we need to be certain in our hearts that we are sure of what we mean when we say the three words the future of civilization rests on—"I love you."

Love From Culture

If we use our culture to arrive at our view of love, we're probably going to have some unnecessary heartbreaks in our life. It's no wonder. The messages about love coming from our culture leave us as bewildered as ever. We live out THE DAYS OF OUR LIVES as THE YOUNG AND THE RESTLESS realizing that we only have ONE LIFE TO LIVE, and AS THE WORLD TURNS we want to search for that GUIDING LIGHT that will keep us from falling in love at a GENERAL HOSPITAL in SANTA BARBARA.

All right . . . you can see I'm having a bit of fun with the daytime TV schedule. Yet the bizarre definitions of "love" portrayed to millions on the daily soap operas are no laughing matter. Like heat at a fruit stand, these daytime dramas accelerate the decay at the core of our cultural values.

Lest you think I'm beyond being "hooked," let me describe an incident on a recent vacation. My wife and I were staying with friends at their summer home in Wyoming. A blue ribbon trout stream snaked its way through the woods and along the fields next to their house. It was irresistible. Whenever the fish were biting, I wanted to be in my waders working my way upstream.

One morning I came back to the house with a basket full of fish and found there was no one there to view my trophies! My friend was still fishing farther up the stream, and the gals had gone to town for groceries. There's nothing more frustrating than looking forward to applause for something I'm only mediocrely gifted at, and end up with nothing. I'd been skunked the day before, so I figured they would go crazy. Depression.

I decided to nurse my disappointment by turning on the tube. Actually, I was bored. If I couldn't have fish tugging on my line or my wife using her eyes to form an exclamation point as I pulled each fish out of my basket, then I was going to fill my time trying to outwit game show contestants.

Because we were so far out in the country, the reception on the television was limited to only a couple of stations. Each was broadcasting a soap opera. It had been some time since I had viewed one of these shows—and they had become a lot more explicit than I remembered! The people on the one I watched had more problems in an hour than I want to have in my entire life. They said the word *love* a lot, but practiced deception, betrayal, anger, and selfishness. I figured this is what the world would be like if only spoiled brats were allowed to fall in love. Everyone took turns either hurting someone or getting hurt.

I couldn't believe anyone would actually watch such a foolish portrayal of life. But the next day I made sure I was out of the stream and into the armchair in time to pick up where all of those selfish, brokenhearted people had let me off the day before. Within three days I was addicted. By the end of the vacation I had a new appreciation for fish. I used to think they were stupid to swallow a lure masquerading as a meal spinning by them in the water. Yet I had done the same thing. Fortunately, I didn't take out a subscription to *Soap Digest*.

People actually take these shows seriously. Sometimes their acceptance borders on the extreme. A pastor friend told me about a lady in his church who had actually requested prayer for one of the couples on her favorite soap. That's like saying Barney Rubble is a great actor. When we can't separate the fiction from the real, we're in trouble.

I know people (lots of them) whose lives seem as if they were scripted by the soap writers. They approach love without a clue to what it is. Their lives are restless and unsatisfied. They keep looking for love in all the wrong places. They are proof that the myths magazines, TV, and movies put forward about love are actually believed.

Remember the definition of love popularized as a result of the movie, *Love Story*? "Love means never having to say you're sorry." It looks nice on a key chain or written cursively across a poster of Ryan O'Neal and Ali McGraw. But if you use it as a guideline for a relationship, you'll probably find yourself disappointed. That's because love means *always* having to say you're sorry (and sometimes even when you haven't done anything wrong). When a person lets a loved one down, he or she should assume responsibility for it.

Our culture throws interference and static at a married couple trying to fine-tune their love. It doesn't make it easy to arrive at accurate conclusions about this mysterious need inside all of us. That's why we must be careful not to allow culture to be an outspoken authority on the subject.

Love From Experience

Culture vies to play a big part in forming our view of love. But its impact is minimal next to the power of experience. What we learn from being loved or being rejected forms the strongest foundation beneath our concepts of love. But here again we run into problems. If experience is our teacher, then we are at the mercy of many variables beyond our control. The parents who reared us, the neighbors who surrounded us, the teachers and religious mentors who influenced us, and the treatment we received in the hands (or the arms) of the people whom we allowed close to us become the confusing impressions that form our understanding of love.

We arrive at the marital altar with a lot of these experiences forming conflicting attitudes. We use the word *love* throughout the wedding ceremony and swear it is the cement bonding our vows. But the married life that follows often reflects that each of us had our own personal definition.

Defining Love

The definition of love we bring to marriage has everything to do with whether or not we are enjoying love. When I visit with a couple struggling in their relationship, I like to ask them to give me their definition of love. My thinking is that if they understand what love is, they are more inclined to achieve it. What I find in almost every case is that both partners have come to the relationship with only the vaguest notion of what love entails.

Think a minute. If you were asked to write out your definition of love, what would you put down? I know that love is one of those dimensions of life that's hard to put into words, but if we are going to be serious about this part of our life, we have to know what we mean when we say, "I love you."

I want to share with you a definition of love that can bring calm to a hurried marriage. It can make a relationship between a husband and wife an oasis in the middle of a thirsty culture. Those who seriously embrace this definition can maintain the ability to love for a lifetime. If a couple loves with this type of love they won't have to face "just divorced" garage sales. They can move beyond today to a lifetime of certainty and contentment.

Let's define love this way:

LOVE IS . . .
THE COMMITMENT OF MY WILL
TO YOUR NEEDS AND BEST INTERESTS
REGARDLESS OF THE COST TO ME.

This is a definition that doesn't bring a bunch of conditions with it. It doesn't require anything from the person being loved. Instead, it is preoccupied with what it can give.

I get a variety of responses when I share this definition with people. Sometimes they say it is exactly the way *they* would define love. Yet a close examination of their lives show that what they believe in theory they don't carry out in practice. Others call the definition "unrealistic," "idealistic," or even "impossible."

I agree that it's not a "natural" way to respond to others, but it is very much an achievable standard for a relationship. Couples who use this as their standard need not fear the present or the future. That's because love which is practiced according to this definition is *secure.* Secure love! Steady, reliable, constant, unshakable, unmovable. Isn't it what our hearts long for? This sort of love is the anchor we throw out when the winds of change shred our sails and the waves of doubt swamp our engines. It's the confidence that comes from being stable during unstable conditions. As marriages throughout America take a fierce beating from culture, couples with secure love can rest in each other's arms. It's this kind of love that turns fear into faith, intimidation into anticipation, worry into wisdom, and failure into success.

As married couples navigate their way through the future, their love for each other may be the only part of their lives that seems permanent. Yet if their love is permanent, they can accept the changes. *Any* changes.

If your love is secure, you can accept anything.

The Power Behind the Love

We are human. We have weaknesses. We bring fragile needs to our marriage relationships. Loving your spouse by committing your will to his or her needs and best interests, regardless of the cost, is SUPERHUMAN. I agree. It just isn't the normal, natural way that people operate. It's a superhuman form of love that comes from the heart of a supernatural God Who made us. If we want to have it toward each other, we must first derive it from God. The husband or wife trying to love without a heart possessed by the Author of Love is going to run out of momentum very quickly—more quickly than he or she would have ever imagined.

Love has a bad habit of giving pop quizzes. When we only have our human resources to draw on, we find ourselves in quick trouble. We need a source of love that knows no boundaries and has no limits. A God who would cross the threshold of time, walk down a back street of civilization, and climb up on a cross that was meant for us knows how to help us love.

Secure love, therefore, requires a secure relationship with the God who is love. This relationship takes a good definition of love and puts *power* behind it. Infinite muscle. It helps us practice in our lives what we intellectually embrace in our hearts.

The Bottom Line

If we have this divine help, then we can begin to implement three crucial ingredients for successful love. These ingredients are:

1. Self-discipline
2. Self-discipline
3. Self-discipline

Actually, they are *self-discipline*, *sensitivity*, and *sacrifice*. But if we aren't willing to discipline our commitment to love . . . sensitivity and sacrifice won't happen anyway. Finding rest in our marriages takes work. It takes a preoccupied commitment to oneness.

Married life in the passing lane provides the ultimate challenge to self-disciplined love. A typical couple faces an array of choices they must make each day if they want to remain committed. There is always something ready to rob us of our time, and someone willing to wedge themselves in between our relationship. Many of the challenges that face us in marriage are good and rewarding, but without discipline to our commitment these challenges can produce a chilling effect on our love.

So we must love with a clear conviction of what we mean by love, and oppose anything or anybody that poses a threat to our marital vows. But even if we win the battle against the external competition, we still have to face the problems within us that make having a rested marriage difficult. It might require a complete retooling of our concept of love and a recommitment to our vows.

One thing we can do is decide in advance that we are going to make a *unilateral commitment* to our spouses. In other words, we are going to fulfill our promises *regardless of what our partners do.* This attitude is not what I hear coming from the weeping wives or hurting husbands who share their pain in counseling. Each has a list of disappointments that serve as the basis for his or her uncommitted behavior. The index finger that points at the errant partner is connected to a broken heart. As the disappointments build, the ability to maintain love drops off.

Unilateral love is another way of saying unconditional love. It's saying to your partner, "I love you, and I'm going to live out this commitment no matter what." You may be reading this and thinking, "Tim, you're dreaming. I could never do that."

I can appreciate that you may have many painful reasons for saying that, but I can assure you that until you make such a commitment, you won't have a relationship that can bring you inner rest. You may have serious hurts—infidelity, betrayal, desertion—that have plagued your marriage in the past. Your reasons for resisting might be strong, but your relationship will never enjoy contentment until you are willing to take the first step of unconditional commitment. You need the same kind of attitude toward your spouse that you have toward your children. Your kids may have disappointed you, betrayed you, or rejected you, but you won't stop loving them.

Once you are prepared to commit to your relationship, the six nonnegotiables necessary for rest that we've discussed in this book become a simple checklist to keep you on target. Maybe a few examples of how to apply these principles will help you see how to make them personal. (Allow me, for our discussion here, to change the order in which they are listed in earlier chapters.)

MANAGING YOUR EXPECTATIONS

If there is any area in our relationship as couples that controls our ability to gain inner rest, I believe it is the expectations we bring to our marriage. As I counsel couples getting married—and couples trying to stay married—this is the one area I emphasize beyond all others.

Two people stand before the preacher with great expectations. This beautiful, intelligent, bright-eyed girl stands hand-in-hand with her strong, courageous, and handsome man. They are going to enjoy a few busy days and rewarding nights before the honeymoon feelings wear off. It may take a year, a month, or twenty-four hours, but they *will* wear off. That's not so bad. Those who preach that every day can be a honeymoon have either never been married or have never been on a honeymoon. Reality is insensitive to the happily-ever-after feelings that fill a couple's heart as they drive from the wedding reception to their first night together.

Reality is going to visit this couple in many ways. Job insecurity, credit card bills, old loves, new loves, dirty diapers, late notices, cold dinners, poorly timed affections, poorly timed headaches, bounced checks, and eventually . . . a chest where their stomach used to be, and nothing where their chest used to be.

This post-honeymoon period is the time when a married couple needs realistic expectations. Unfortunately, these new pressures usually reveal the opposite.

I'll make this real simple. What most of us do when we come to a relationship is develop a formula for success that assumes our partner will act, think, and respond in certain ways. *That is why most of us become disappointed with our spouses.* We are expecting that individual to fulfill our formula for happiness. That's fine if they're cooperative. Unfortunately, we marry humans, not robots. We marry people with minds of their own—and their own set of unrealistic expectations!

When our partner doesn't fulfill the expectations of our formula for success we panic. Some people try to muscle their spouse into cooperating with their formula. This always backfires. Others give in. Too many give up.

There is a way to counter all of this. It's going to sound farfetched to a lot of you, but believe me, it's the only way a couple can bring rest to their relationship. What I need to do is come to a relationship with expectations that only cover *me*. After all, I'm the only person over whom I have control. I don't control my wife. I don't want to. Even if I wanted to, I can't. She's an individual with a mind of her own.

Instead of making her actions a requirement for my success, I want to make my actions a commitment to *her* success. In other words, if my contentment is contingent on her cooperation, I'm sure to lack contentment. If, however, my contentment is wrapped up in bringing to my marriage all that I can offer without *requiring* anything in return, I am more likely to enjoy peace in my marriage. I shift my spouse from being the accommodator of my needs to being the object of my love.

Bringing rest to a distracted and hurried marriage means managing my expectations of the relationship. If my formula for being fulfilled in my love is knowing that I have committed my will to the needs and best interests of my spouse, no matter what the cost, then I can control that. If she doesn't respond back, I can still experience the rest that comes from knowing I've done my part. But if she responds back with a similar attitude toward me, our marriage is doubly blessed.

A Reconciled Heart

Marriages can't handle the long-term pressure of bitterness. Husbands and wives hurt each other. Sometimes it's accidental, other times it's intended. Regardless, individuals desiring rest in their marriage must be prepared to forgive. They must be willing to crumble up their list of hurts and throw it in the trash can at the foot of the cross.

I know some people can list hurts that seem beyond forgiveness. That's why forgiveness must come through God's power. It is the only way to put rest where bitterness once festered. It is a gift we can give to our spouses, but it is also a gift we give to ourselves. It means we are willing to do something about the anger in our hearts. It's a way of disciplining our love and bringing rest to our spirits.

Living Within the Limits

A professor from one of our nation's more respected seminaries was being interviewed on "The Phil Donahue Show." He shared that he had a great marriage with his wife of twenty-five-plus years. In the process of the conversation he said that one of the reasons he felt their marriage was strong was because of their sexual relationship. However, when he let the viewing audience peek into the privacy of their bedroom, people were surprised to see that this couple shared their bed and their sexual relationship with someone else.

This theologian was proud of the fact that he always brought his latest edition of *Penthouse* to bed with him. He would stretch Miss Whoever out on the bed next to his wife. There was no comparison. The one-dimensional playmate became the real object of his affections. His wife was only there to complete the fantasy. He made love to two women at the same time—the wife in his arms and the airbrushed centerfold in his head.

This couple was living a lie. This husband was defrauding his wife by not accepting her for who she was. He was only using her while filling his mind with images she could never fulfill.

No marriage can survive without boundaries. Anyone who says otherwise is dreaming. A river without boundaries is a swamp. Swamps stink. A marriage that wants security and rest must recognize that there are clear boundaries when we deal with one another. These boundaries aren't there to fence in our freedom but to fence out those pressures and people that would seek to steal our freedom.

A partner who turns to an affair to provide the missing magic his or her marriage has lost is practicing cruel self-deception. Affairs *don't* work. The excitement is transitory—soon overwhelmed with emptiness and regret.

When God said don't covet someone else's property, don't commit adultery, and don't steal, He said it because He knew what disciplined love requires. Those who willingly submit their thoughts and actions to the clear boundaries God outlines in the Scriptures say "I love you" in one of the most genuine ways possible.

An Eternal Perspective

Our commitments to each other in marriage are "until death us do part." But even though our marriages end, we don't. The soul of an individual is eternal. The apostle Paul told husbands that they have a responsibility to their wives that ends when they die, but is realized when they meet the Lord. We are to love them and live with them in such a way that they can come to God "holy and blameless" (Ephesians 5:27).

Keeping in mind that the person is *eternal* who sleeps next to you at night and eats across the table from you each day, has a way of changing the way you treat that individual. Honoring, affirming, and cherishing become a greater desire when we know it can become part of a gift package to God in eternity.

Serving While Suffering

Sidney would come home from work drained. But three hungry children had to be fed. Over the years he had become fairly efficient. Little, eager hands would do a childish job of setting the table while his tired hands worked over the stove. Laughs and lectures would make the dinner ritual more than substance for the body—it was also an investment in a lifetime.

Dishes would be washed, clean pajamas would replace the clothes that bore the marks of a day of adventures, and stories and prayers would help sleepy eyes drift from the cares of the day to the quiet and safety of slumber.

That's when Sidney would retire to the back corner of the house. He'd say goodbye to the day nurse and then complete the rest of his evening ritual. A catheter bag had to be emptied and a bed pan had to be offered. He would take a clean wash cloth and warm water to wash the face of his bride. It had been a couple of years since the accident. Yet his vows were clear: "For better or for worse." It could have been him who had been hit by the drunk. Instead, it was the woman he loved.

He would tell her all the good things about his day, never the worries. He knew that she loved music, so he'd hum her a few tunes from their past. Then he'd look into her eyes and tell her what he told her every night before she went to sleep and every morning when she woke up.

"I love you, honey. You're my life, my love, and my wife."

He had regrets, sure. But no complaints. Although his life was different and difficult, he could live it with a rested spirit. He understood that rest sometimes requires us to serve when we suffer.

MANAGING YOUR GIFTS

A marriage in search of rest must learn how to discipline its gifts and assets. The people who make up the marriage—and the children that union creates—represent the greatest treasures of all. We must manage those treasures well.

There is a practical way this works out in a marriage. If a husband is frivolous with his money and slothful with his talent, he makes a statement to his wife. He's saying, "Your security isn't that important to me—*you* aren't that important to me." If a man won't stick with a job and can't keep his checkbook reconciled, he is going to rob his wife of rest.

When a wife who doesn't have to work outside the home neglects the house and doesn't maintain the household possessions, she is saying to her husband, "I don't value what you provide—therefore, I don't value who you are."

Managing the gifts that God has given us personally and as a couple requires serious discipline. Failure to be conscientious in this area of our relationship is guaranteed to add much pain and restlessness to it.

With the world spinning so fast and friendships being so few, a marriage may be the only stable and secure commitment a couple will know throughout their hurried life. It must be put on a higher priority if a person wants to enjoy rest over the long haul.

John Fischer, a Christian musician, offers some sound advice along these lines. It seems that John had rented a room from an elderly couple who had been married longer than most people get a chance to live. But even though time had wrinkled their hands, stooped their posture, and slowed them down, it hadn't diminished the excitement and love they felt toward each other. John could tell that their love had not stopped growing since the day of their wedding—over a half century before.

Intrigued, the singer finally had an opportunity to ask the old man the secret to his success as a husband.

"Oh," said the old gentleman with a twinkle in his eye, "that's simple. Just bring her roses on Wednesday— she never expects them then."

The conversation inspired a song—and a fitting way to end this chapter.

> Give her roses on Wednesday, when everything is blue,
> Roses are red and your love must be new.
> Give her roses on Wednesday, keep it shining through,
> Love her when love's the hardest thing to do.
>
> Love isn't something you wait for,
> Like some feeling creeping up from behind.
> Love's a decision to give more,
> And keep giving all of the time.
>
> Give her roses on Wednesday . . .
>
> It's easy to love when it's easy,
> When you're in a Friday frame of mind.
> But loving when living gets busy,
> Is what love was waiting for all the time.
>
> Give her roses on Wednesday . . . [12]

CHAPTER 11

Giving the Gift of Rest to Your Children

My everyday life is filled with visual reminders of priorities. The soap-written message scribbled on the bathroom mirror reminds me that I've got a breakfast appointment. The claim check my wife has wedged into the crease in my steering wheel reminds me that I have to pick up the dry cleaning on the way home from the office. I can't even start my car without it reminding me that I may have an accident and I'd probably be glad that I put on my seat belt.

There's something about routine that makes us humans prone to forgetfulness. Even though three little children run and play throughout my house every day, it's easy to get so distracted by the madness of my daily responsibilities that I forget how much of my attention they need. "Out of sight, out of mind" became a cliché because it's true. Because I spend a lot of the day at my office, it's easy to find myself making my children a *compartment* of my life rather than the *essence*.

In my desperation to remember my priorities, I have set six individually framed pictures across the upper shelf of my rolltop desk at work. The picture on the left is of the Jameson Memorial Hospital in New Castle, Pennsylvania. That's where I was born. The picture on the right is of a six-foot-high granite monument that stands in the middle of the Graceland Cemetery just outside of this same town. You can't miss the word "Kimmel" carved on its side. The earth beneath it conceals the remains of several generations of my family. The four pictures that sit between these two outer pictures are of Darcy (my wife), Karis, Cody, and Shiloh.

What we do for a living has a way of absorbing our attention. Its demands are so great and its ego satisfaction so intoxicating that it can easily become the focus of our lives. I love my work, but I don't want it to become the heart of my existence—my reason for living. That's why I have those pictures strategically placed on my desk. When I look up from my studies, I come eye level with a reminder of my purpose. Stealing a peek at them several times a day has a way of keeping my work (and my life) in proper perspective. In the brief moment it takes me to scan them I receive a message in the cluttered back rooms of my brain.

The pictures say, "Don't forget, Tim, *this* is where you checked in (the hospital), *this* is where you're checking out (the cemetery), and *these four people* in the middle *are why you are here.*"

My job as a parent is a temporary responsibility with eternal consequences. The amount of time that my wife and I have to adequately develop a sense of inner security and personal adequacy within our children is fleeting. Incredibly brief. They are only in our home for about twenty years. And since they are going to sleep, eat, and go to school during most of that time, we need to wisely use the small amount of time left.

But our lives are cluttered with choices and distractions that make giving priority to our children difficult. We need to remind ourselves every day that the time we have to pass on a heritage of rest and calm is quickly dwindling away.

We have to be deliberate about our commitment to them if we ever want to meet their inner needs for love, purpose, and hope. By giving them these gifts, we equip them for life. Children who know they are loved, know they have a purpose, and know they have a hope are prepared for anything this world wants to dish up. A secure, loving home is the only environment that naturally satisfies these needs.

As Laurens van der Post and Jane Taylor said in their anthropological study, *Testament to the Bushmen*, "No culture has ever been able to provide a better shipyard for building storm-proof vessels for the journey of man from the cradle to the grave than the individual nourished in a loving family."[13]

Secure and loving homes don't just happen. The competition for time and concentration is too intense. If parents want their children to be raised in an environment that produces calm and confidence, they're going to have to work overtime to make it happen.

PRIORITIES FOR PARENTING

Because our hurried lives have a way of stealing our attention, we need to make a calculated effort to maintain priorities that will give our children the best possible chance of achieving security and significance as adults.

There are two priorities every parent should be careful not to neglect. Others could be mentioned, but when it comes to giving rest to your children, these are the ones from which you'll derive the most help.

The first priority is PREPARATION. We must always keep in mind that our job as parents is to prepare our children to live independently of us. Before they move out from under our influence they must be adequately prepared to face the best and worst that life may bring their way. There will always be lessons for them to learn as adults, but before they leave our home they must have the fundamental disciplines of their life developed enough to adapt and survive in an adult's world.

If we are to prepare them to leave, then we must be prepared to let them go. Too often, the adolescent child is prepared to leave, but the parent refuses to cut the cords to set him free. Parents who keep their children in a position of dependence, or who refuse to back out of their lives as the children reach adulthood do more damage than they could ever imagine.

Once our children get out of college, we need to move from being a *resource* to being a *reference*. We offer advice when solicited. This forces our children to stand on their own two feet. If we indefinitely bankroll them, we keep them in neutral. They need to start stumbling and getting up on their own if we ever expect them to run with the pack.

The following analogy may be a bit worn, but its truth is fresh. When a mother eagle builds her nest, she structures the frame out of thorns and twisted limbs. She pads this thorny nest with down and feathers. As the eaglets hatch and mature they enjoy the comfort and warmth of their feathered nest. But as they reach maturity, the mother eagle has to take deliberate measures to get them to jump out and fly. That's when she starts to remove the down that pads the nest. The young eagles become more and more interested in flying as the nest gets more and more uncomfortable.

She wants them to soar to great heights as adults. That's what good parents want for their children. But it will never happen if we don't prepare them for independence.

It's good to communicate this to our children as they grow up. We need to let them know what we are doing and why we are doing it. When they know that instruction and activity in the present is going to serve them in the future, they feel confident. We give them rest because they know we are taking the worry out of growing up and moving on.

When your children are young, simple chores can become excellent opportunities to let them know you are preparing them to be successful adults. If they're helping you cook, you can let them know this skill will serve them well when they are out on their own. As you are helping them clean their rooms you can encourage them that they're learning how to be good managers of their own homes someday.

Anything you do to prepare them for the future is a way of saying "I love you."

Preparation, then, helps parents meet the requirements for giving rest to their children. But preparation, by itself, isn't enough. We need a second priority for giving rest to our children.

This is the priority of PROTECTION.

Life can be harsh on children. They are defenseless when it comes to competing with the philosophies and forces within a culture that would seek to harm or mislead them.

Parents play a critical role in protecting their offspring from these cultural pressures. Our job is to run interference for our children, to lead them. They need to know we will fight the battles they are unprepared to face. They gain inner confidence in knowing we will do the providing, the worrying, and the struggling until they are ready to do it themselves.

All along we are preparing them to be able to protect themselves. These two priorities, then, accommodate each other. We protect them by preparing them, and we prepare them by protecting them.

A FOUR-DIMENSIONAL CHECKLIST

There are different dimensions that make up a child's personality: the *physical* dimension, the *emotional* dimension, the *intellectual* dimension, and the *spiritual* dimension. If we want to do a good job of giving rest to our children, we have to help them in all four dimensions. Batting three-for-four may be great in baseball, but in trying to raise children, it's simply not good enough. A child needs help in all four areas if he wants to enjoy a balanced attitude toward life.

Restlessness has a way of creeping in through the unlocked doors of our personality. Leaving a child's personality unguarded is an open invitation to frustration, heartache, and pain.

With this in mind, let's think through our four-point checklist. With each dimension we need to consider how we can both *prepare* and *protect* our child so that he or she can enjoy the maximum amount of calm and confidence on the journey into adulthood.

Rest for the Body

Some kids lack inner rest simply because they lack physical rest. Children don't naturally know how to monitor their energy levels as an adult would. Instead of pacing themselves, they will literally run until they drop. There are times when that's okay. If our children are having a lot of fun playing in the backyard, we may choose to forego their naps. But we must compensate by putting them to bed early. Children need that kind of physical supervision to make sure they develop adequate rest habits. A student who works hard in school, over-prepares his homework, and maintains a busy social calendar sometimes needs a parent to call "time out." He needs to be reminded that bodies have limits, and those who push themselves pay too high a price.

We cannot assume that he has thought that through. It may never have occurred to him!

Another area in which parents can play a big role is in a child's diet. A child who is not taught how to eat properly and maintain his weight is going to struggle all of his life. By not helping our kids in this area, we are setting them up for lots of frustration and anxiety. And the physical difficulties brought on by poor eating habits often prove to be minor compared to the emotional hurts that come with being overweight.

The bottom line is that we need to help our children make proper choices when it comes to their bodies. It will protect them now and it will prepare them for tomorrow. In the meantime they will experience the joy of being at rest inside because they have the outside under control.

Rest for the Emotions

I wish there was a way to hook a sign on every kid's chest just above the heart that said: HANDLE WITH CARE, FRAGILE EMOTIONS ON BOARD. I honestly can't believe how careless some parents can be with their children's emotions. They thoughtlessly presume that kids have sophisticated emotions capable of processing input at a mature adult level. They're wrong. Dead wrong! But too often, before they figure it out, the damage has been done.

A parent can crush a child's spirit with a glance or a few poorly chosen words. I've done that. But the fact is that their young emotions are delicate, and we need to be careful how we handle them. Since children are a responsibility from God, we are called to steward them well. We are going to be just as responsible for how we stewarded our children's emotions as we are for how we stewarded our money.

How can we make sure that we are preparing our children emotionally? There are several ways, but let me simply mention a few.

One thing we can do is teach them the purpose of emotions. It is crucial that you teach a child that emotions are for *feeling* not for *thinking*. This may seem obvious, but my experience in counseling is that too many people call on their emotions to do critical thinking. This always leads to trouble because emotions are not equipped for those sorts of demands.

Emotions only know how to feel—and don't even have to tell the truth. Emotions are free agents. They can do anything they want. You might be at a friend's birthday party and not be able to stop crying. You might be at a funeral and not be able to stop laughing. You think you're going crazy when all that is really happening is that you are experiencing the effects of emotions with a mind of their own.

If we don't teach our children how to recognize the proper use of their emotions, they could be tempted to call on them to do their reasoning for them. That's the surest way to create a person plagued by impulsiveness. People who think with their emotions can end up spending their lives fighting problems with debt, divorce, promiscuity, and job instability. In other words, they are guaranteed restlessness.

Our children need to learn how to allow their emotions freedom of expression while avoiding the temptation to use them as the basis for making vital decisions. Our children need to see us pull back from the feelings that surround a major decision long enough and far enough to appraise it objectively. We shouldn't buy high-ticket items on a whim. We shouldn't pass judgment on people with only first impressions. Kids need to see parents processing life through intellect, as well as emotions.

A second way parents can help give rest to their children's emotions is by giving them the gift of tears. Tears free up a languishing spirit by providing an outlet of relief.

I listened recently to a pastor talking about one of the saddest events in our nation's history. Most people who watched the funeral of President Kennedy remember the strength that little "John-John" Kennedy showed as the casket of his father lay in front of him. Before he saluted the casket, however, John-John was fighting tears. His little heart wanted to wail. He was informed, however, that he was a Kennedy, and "Kennedys don't cry!"

If Kennedys were born with tear ducts, then Kennedys were meant to cry. Tears can be a companion through the dark hours and a comfort when words and affections fail. Our children, both *boys* and girls, must not be discouraged from crying, because crying is a significant way to bring rest to their emotions.

The same could be said for laughter! Smiles and laughter are natural inclinations. But insensitivity and bitterness can wipe the smile off a child's face forever. When we fill our children's days with laughter, we medicate their emotions. We introduce them to an internal friend that will be loyal to them all of their lives.

Another way that parents can give rest to their children's emotions is by displaying affection. Children receive more confidence from a hug than they do from a good grade on their report card. They get more mileage out of a compliment than they do out of an expensive store-bought gift. Affections—meaningful touch and affirming words—form a wall of protection around a child's confidence. It's hard to feel insignificant when a mother and father are generous with affection.

Meaningful affections are the best way to protect your son or daughter from sexual pressures in the future. A child who is starving for affection is a lot more inclined to succumb to physical temptation than one who regularly receives meaningful touch and compliments.

Preparing and protecting your child's emotions is an investment in your grandchildren! Ever thought of that? Stable and secure emotions have a way of reproducing themselves.

Emotions that are guarded and guided by loving parents are emotions that will hold up against an angry world. They are emotions that will enjoy honest expression when they are called on to celebrate at the wedding of a friend, worry at the side of a sick child, or moan over the casket of a mate. Conscientious parenting calls us to give the sweet sense of rest to our children's emotions.

Rest for the Mind

Most parents would say they do a fairly decent job of preparing their children intellectually. That's because we assume that "a good education" is our child's biggest requirement for intellectual competence.

Unfortunately, a good education only guarantees that a child has mental skills. It says that he can compete in the arenas that are branches of his training. But we all know that education doesn't transfer calm. Some of the most educated people who have ever lived make the best case studies for depression and anxiety. Rest is not a product of education.

Parents, however, who see the link between logical thinking and rest go to work helping their children learn how to use their intellect to overcome restlessness. Common sense is not genetic. It is a skill picked up by observation. When children see us use common sense to solve problems, to overcome prejudice, to choose right and avoid wrong, they feel a confidence building inside of them. That's because common sense keeps us out of trouble; it keeps us from living life at the extremes. Extremes clutter a life with anger, feelings of superiority, and isolation. People who live balanced lives can find rest more often and more easily.

But common sense parenting recognizes that even though education doesn't guarantee rest, it does guarantee a better opportunity for gainful employment. Being able to make a living and compete in the future is going to have a lot of bearing on our children's sense of calm and confidence once they are adults. The high-tech world waiting for the new generation of students to graduate isn't going to be very sympathetic to the unprepared. The adults of tomorrow are going to have to be able to not only think intellectually, but logically.

Parents serious about giving their children intellectual rest have got to be prepared to help them. Children need coaching, tutoring, and discipline to gain the skills needed to be balanced. Parents who do a thorough job of educating their children have to be committed to sacrifice. The work that is required to produce intellectual discipline is seldom innate within a child. It has to be developed in him.

While we're on the subject of intellectual discipline,

I observe some parents going to two dangerous extremes. One extreme is that of overachievement. Straight A's, honor rolls, dean's lists and awards are overemphasized. A parent may *say* that he only expects a child to do his best, but the child is watching the nonverbal cues, too. He knows when parents make "achievement" the key to affirmation and affection.

Driven, overachieving parents have a bad habit of passing on their bad habits. There is no rest for a driven heart. Kids who pick up driven habits are more likely to spend all the extra money they make from their achievements paying bills at the cardiac care unit or the psychiatric ward. Pushing a child toward excellence for the sake of excellence is a betrayal. We need to draw them to their best, not push them beyond their limit.

The other extreme that I see some parents take is in focusing a child's intellectual training in one area to the exclusion of others. Some do this because of a particular interest of their own. But others "guard" their child from a broad education because they are afraid of exposing their child's mind to certain myths or lies within a given field of academics.

I agree that children need to be protected from some teachings. But we must be selective in our protection. In their zeal to protect their children, some parents unwittingly leave them ill-equipped to weigh information critically. The unfortunate result is that our children can become trapped by the very myths and lies we were trying to keep them from embracing. A good, balanced exposure to fine arts, literature, history, and science—with a loving parent looking over the child's shoulder—can help resolve this dilemma.

Involved parents can help their children weigh the problem areas of education. Parents who take time to help their children consider potential threats to a developing value system come closer to preparing them to stand on their own. Open-minded people are often too vulnerable to deception, but closed-minded people can be dangerous. What we need are parents who stand for a value system and take the time to transfer it to their child's intellect. That produces balanced children who can enjoy rest in crucial areas of their lives.

Rest for the Spirit

The greatest asset a parent can give his or her children is a spiritual heritage. Children need to know they are supremely loved by a personal God. They need to rest in the eternal security found in a personal relationship with Jesus Christ.

I'm shocked how often and how badly parents drop the ball in this dimension. It's almost as if they don't acknowledge the spiritual dimension's existence.

When I was a youth pastor at my local church, we had a young man come to visit our Wednesday evening Bible study. He was looking for some answers to big questions in his life. You could tell there was a void in his heart needing to be filled by God.

After visiting us for a few weeks he made a decision to give his life to God. I prayed with him and gave him a Bible. We chatted at length before he went home to tell the good news to his parents.

About eleven o'clock that night I received a call from an angry mother. She had venom in her voice as she worked me over verbally. She claimed that we were shoving religion down her son's throat—that he was too young to understand how to believe in a God whom he couldn't see. She further said that she wanted her son to be open-minded—not limited to one concept of God.

After ventilating her anger, she stopped a moment to catch her breath. I thought, *My turn!*

"Excuse me, ma'am, but did you teach Calvin about Santa Claus when he was little?"

The answer was indignant. "Of course, I did."

"Did he believe in him?"

"Yes."

"So much for the argument that children can't believe in something they can't see. Let me ask another question. Do you think table manners are important?"

"Yes."

"Did you insist on Calvin observing good manners at the table as he grew up?"

"Yes."

"Why?"

"I wanted him to know how to behave properly at the table."

"Good. That was wise. But you know, I find it interesting that you could be so dogmatic about table manners, and yet so threatened when your son becomes concerned about his destiny."

This mother ultimately withdrew her boy from church and discouraged him from pursuing any spiritual heritage. Calvin is in his mid-twenties now. He's failed at marriage and fights deeply embedded suicidal tendencies.

People are eternal just as certainly as they are physical. Because of that fact, we must not deny our children's legitimate need for eternal answers.

A strong biblical education taught in the context of a supportive loving family is the greatest gift a child could ever receive. It is the gift of rest, wrapped in its most beautiful and permanent package.

Our children need church, the Bible, and prayer from the leadership of parents who embrace these elements themselves. This will provide the main ingredient needed for completing the physical, emotional, and intellectual dimensions of their life—THE TRUTH. Jesus said, "You shall know the truth, and the truth shall set you free" (John 8:32).

PREPARATION FOR LIFE'S FRONT LINES

There is one young man who knows the power that can be found in a Christian heritage. Dr. Billy Kim, a leading minister from South Korea, shared a powerful story that came from the shadows of one of Korea's darkest hours.

Heartbreak Ridge stretches east to west along the thirty-ninth parallel dividing North and South Korea. The ridged rocks making up this mountain range look like gigantic shark's teeth from a distance. The mountain got its name from the battles that were fought near its peak.

During the Korean War, Heartbreak Ridge was bathed in the blood and tears of thousands of American and U.N. soldiers.

One night the battle was unusually intense. The North Koreans were firmly dug in to the rock. Their positions gave them a home court advantage against the Allied troops. They kept the night skies lit with flares and the air filled with bullets.

One American soldier worked his way through the maze of enemy emplacements only to be struck down about fifty meters beyond the enemy's outer lines.

Out in the darkness he screamed in pain, begging for someone to rescue him.

Nobody moved.

It was attempted murder for him to call for help, and anyone coming to his rescue was committing suicide.

His moans and cries for help continued—unheeded.

One young man, crouched in a foxhole, kept his head down but kept lifting his wrist up into the light given off by the flares. Suddenly he bolted. Slithering and crawling, he followed the screams until he found his wounded comrade. He grunted and dragged until he was able to pull the soldier back through the enemy lines to the safety of an American foxhole.

His sergeant came crawling in to find out what gave him the sudden urge for heroics.

"What in the world got into you?" he asked. "Why did you take the risk?"

"It wasn't really a risk," the young man replied. "I kept checking my watch until I knew it was safe. You see, Sarge, I left on the hour, because it was 9:00 A.M. back home in Kansas. My mom told me before I left that she'd be praying for me every morning at nine o'clock. I knew that God would protect me."

Do you want to give your children rest for their spirits? Become a parent who prays for them every day. Give them the biblical leadership that hands them a spiritual heritage.

THE PAINFUL TRUTH

Now, for the hard part.

As I conclude this chapter, I'm reluctant to share a conviction that I have about all of this. I'm reluctant because I know that too many parents don't want to hear what I'm about to say. Because they don't want to hear it, they begin the process of rationalization, finding fault with the person making the bold and convicting statements.

I'm going to state my conviction anyway. I'm not doing this because I'm brave. Frankly, the reactions that some people have to this conviction intimidates the heck out of me. I'm not into martyrdom. I'm saying it because the battle for the hearts of our children is being lost, and we can't afford to allow this to happen.

Here goes.

The type of parenting I've outlined is not idealistic. Nor is it unrealistic. It's the BOTTOM LINE. To do it right takes YEARS of TIME.

Dads, if we think we can be effective fathers while at the same time spending seventy-five to ninety-five hours a week climbing the ladder of success, we're kidding ourselves. If we think we can dump the responsibility of raising our children off on our partner while we hide behind the "bread winner" mask, we're hallucinating. Being an effective father requires personal involvement. We cannot—we dare not—delegate our parenting responsibilities to someone else and feel that we have fulfilled our calling to our children. It just doesn't work.

Moms, the painful truth for you is that producing

secure, confident children takes a lot of hands-on attention. No one is better equipped to mother your children than you. The issue of working outside the home glares into the face of the modern mother. For some, there is no choice—you're divorced, you're widowed, or your husband is unemployed. Perhaps you'd like to be home, but you can't.

Most working moms, however, aren't making their decision from that position.

Work, with it's ego benefits and extra income, must be weighed against the long-term needs of our children. When it comes to this issue, there are no easy answers. Loving takes time and time requires sacrifice—somewhere. It gets painful when the sacrifices cut into lifestyle. The lifestyle sacrifices don't have to be *forever*, but they may have to be for *now*.

Effective parenting cannot be done by accident. We have to parent on purpose.

Those couples who are willing to swim against the current tide of cultural pressure are going to have a reward waiting for them. They may not be able to dress as well, drive as nice a car, go out as much, or have as nice a house as those who ride with the contemporary flow. But they will have the blessing of knowing they gave their kids what their kids needed most—THEIR PARENTS' ATTENTION.

When we stand before God someday, we're going to have to give an account. We may have chosen, as moms and dads, to let someone else do the bulk of the rearing and value programming of our children. But it is we who will have to give an account for our children.

You may want to throw down the book at this point and forget everything we've discussed. I hope you don't. Give it some time to work in your heart. Think about it . . . pray about it.

Give your kids your best shot.

CHAPTER 12

Maintaining Rest in the Work Arena

W HILE speaking at a conference in Texas, I met a man whose life served as a universal illustration of the frustration of maintaining rest in the work arena. He started talking to me while we were standing in a crowd just outside the conference center. By the way he kept strolling away from the group, I could tell that he wanted a private conversation.

There was a dock overlooking a lake about a hundred feet away, so I grabbed a couple of lawn chairs and set them up just out of hearing distance toward the end of the dock. He sat for a few minutes small-talking about his family before he moved to the issue on his heart.

He was a salesman. It came to him naturally. He had been with his company several years and had enjoyed an admirable track record and a lucrative income. But he had run into a slump.

"Aren't slumps part of the territory?" I asked him.

He agreed. But this slump had shown him something. It had uncovered the nature of the system in which he found himself caught up.

He explained how his sales office operated. There was an executive office with paneled walls, plush carpet, nice paintings, and a beautiful desk. A metal sleeve was screwed on the door so that the occupant of this office could slide in his or her name plate. Along with it came the use of a personal secretary to help with appointments and correspondence. This was the royal treatment that the Sales Leader of the Month enjoyed. This office had been his home most of the months he worked for his company. His million dollar sales plaques seldom had to be taken off the wall in order to make way for a new leader.

The rest of the office was an open area with cubicles and phones. The other salespeople made their appointments from these desks and shared a secretarial pool.

Over in the corner, near the door where workers passed in and out of the room, there was a card table. It was for the salesperson with the poorest sales record each month. It had a pay phone hanging on the wall next to it.

This had been his "office" for the past three months.

He had a lot of financial responsibilities that he had to maintain. He was working harder than ever, but things simply weren't happening for him. His wife was patient, but worried. His kids were understanding, but neglected. His boss was encouraging, but getting desperate. Anyone who occupied the "loser of the month" desk for four months was automatically terminated. Company policy.

Even with this hanging over his head, he had chosen to stick with his vacation plans and take his family to their annual week of family camp. But he was finding it impossible to concentrate on the speakers or enjoy the activities with his family knowing that he might return to work the following Monday to find his sales awards and million dollar plaques sitting in a cardboard box next to the exit.

I asked him about the alternatives. Like getting another job. He said that he could but didn't feel that it would change the bigger problem.

The bigger problem was *success*. He wanted it, he needed it, but he was tired of the demands it made on him and his family.

In his line of work, success was tangible. You could count it, look at it, live in it, polish it, drive it, wear it, or play with it. Without meaning to, he had fallen victim to a system that measures a person's value in accomplishments. He couldn't fault the "system" for using accomplishments as a measuring stick for rewards. But when he allowed himself to step over the line and use accomplishments as a yardstick for measuring his own value, he got caught in the trap.

The trap is the "success fantasy" . . . the arbitrary but deliberate standard the work arena uses to motivate and control people. The young man sitting at the edge of a dock in Texas was living the same nightmare experienced by men and women all over the country. He was shell-shocked from salvos the system fires at the unproductive, and yet found himself equally fatigued when he was "leading the charge."

Advising him to find another line of work wouldn't solve the bigger problem. He could become a landscaper or a painter, but the environment in which he would work still uses the same yardstick for measuring a person's value. Whether you are a teacher, technician, construction worker, preacher, doctor, lawyer, or Indian Chief, your job offers a hand-polished desk in a private office or a card table with a pay phone. They may not be physical, but they are no less real.

A leading NBC correspondent was addressing a luncheon of business men and women. During his career with NBC he had enjoyed the luxury of working out of the Washington, D.C. bureau—in touch with some of the most significant news stories of the century. Almost daily he found himself walking up and down the corridors of power. He candidly described the emotions that went through his head when he found that he had been fired from his job. One day he had a White House pass and could walk into the press briefing room any time he wanted . . . and the very next day he found himself in the unemployment office sitting next to a black truck driver with mud on his boots.

Though the unemployed truck driver had always been his equal, the journalist had worked in an arena that led him to believe he was superior. When he took his turn working at the metaphorical card table and pay phone, it cut him up inside. But it also showed him how insecure life in the paneled office can be.

Work and the money we receive from it are the greatest contributors to restless and hurried lifestyles. They are also the hardest ones to bring under control. They go hand in hand. How we view one will determine how we handle the other.

It's easy to feel like a hostage when it comes to these two areas of your life. Even people with the finest priorities and the best intentions find themselves in a struggle. Money and work are necessities. But they make selfish demands and don't have much concern for our needs. You can find yourself at their mercy in an instant.

I'm like you. I want to take adequate care of my family. I'd like to engage in "meaningful" work. I'd like to be able to dream a little and plan a little. There's nothing wrong with these things. But I live in a culture that wants to program my dreams and manipulate my plans. The world in which I earn a living doesn't always share my convictions as a husband and a father, and has a bad habit of withholding rewards from people who maintain biblical priorities toward money.

When it comes to money and work, the average family feels handcuffed to an attitude that has no regard for their inner need for calm and confidence. Anxiety hits them as they dress for work on Monday morning. It jumps out at them when they total their monthly bills and see that the balance in the checkbook isn't as big as the total of their deficits. They are either anxious because they are struggling to get ahead or they are anxious because they are groping to get by. They are seldom granted the luxury of enjoying a position somewhere in between these two nerve-racking extremes.

WHAT PRICE EXCELLENCE?

Tom Peters is the co-author of two of the most widely read books on the subject of work in the twentieth century. His second book, *A Passion For Excellence*, sets forth the mandates for excellence in the work arena. He's emphatic about the need for prioritizing the customer, backing up your product with thorough service, and working from the strength of integrity. He draws his discussion of excellence to a conclusion by talking about its cost.

An honest but alarming statement appears in the last page of the last chapter of the book.

> We are frequently asked if it is possible to "have it all"—a full and satisfying personal life and a full and satisfying, hard-working professional one. Our answer is: No. The price of excellence is time, energy, attention and focus, at the very same time that energy, attention and focus could have gone toward enjoying your daughter's soccer game. Excellence is a high cost item.[14]

> As David Ogilvy observed in *Confessions of an Advertising Man*: "If you prefer to spend all your spare time growing roses or playing with your children, I like you better, but do not complain that you are not being promoted fast enough."[15]

Divorce, angry kids, and failing health are not the assumed requirements for success, but they are too often the product. Company presidents may talk about the importance of the family. They may say they are committed to their employees' marriages and kids, but the actual posture of the top brass is seen on promotion day, awards day, or payday. A man who doesn't want to work overtime on Saturday because his son has a Little League game is made to feel guilty. If you pass up a promotion because you said it would be too demanding on your marriage, you are considered unambitious. Like it or not, being successful at work and being successful at home is a difficult fence to straddle.

The nightmare increases if the family embraces the same standards for measuring success in the home as those in the work arena. It's so easy to buy into the myths that bigger is better, significance can be determined by superiority, or that security can be bought. It drives families to determine their value by their position on the social ladder, by the labels inside their clothing, by the square footage of their home, or by the bottom line on their investments.

We do this because it is the outspoken message of our environment. Our world makes it clear that the successful man or woman can't accept second best. They can't put ceilings on their ambition. The fastest way to end up in last place is to say that you're satisfied with second place. With all of this bombarding the American family, it's no wonder the average home has credit cards at their limit, a mortgage they can't afford, both spouses working, and no time to get acquainted with each other.

WHAT PRICE COURAGE?

What we need to enjoy rest in our work is not success, but *courage*. Success, as the world understands it, is out of our control and just beyond our reach. Because success is determined by shifting external standards, we may achieve it tomorrow only to find it redefined the day after. Courage, however, does not require plaques, promotions, or pedigree. But if it becomes an attitude that we bring toward our work, it can reward us with rest, confidence, and calm.

I have a close friend whose father, Jim, didn't set out to be a success. He didn't plan on being a hero either. He turned out to be both. He did it with courage.

The world was at war. Red flags with swastikas and white flags with a red sun in the middle flapped in the breeze over lands they had no prior claim to. German soldiers were entrenched throughout Europe and Japanese soldiers were entrenched on islands in the South Pacific. The United States joined the other countries of the world to do something about it.

That's how Jim found himself on the inside of amphibious landing equipment—four times. The battles to liberate the islands of the South Pacific started offshore as terrified young men climbed down into the insides of these attack vessels. Some went once, and a few went twice, but seldom did anyone hit the beach four times. They usually didn't live long enough to have the privilege.

Jim joined thousands of men like him in facing a common enemy. He shared their fears and anxieties.

He wanted to succeed in overcoming the enemy, but knew that the outcome of the battle was not under his control. He could neither manipulate the enemy nor wield a great deal of control over his fellow marines.

But he did have control over himself.

So he brought to the battle the vital necessity for personal calm and ultimate victory. He brought courage.

General Ulysses S. Grant has been attributed with the statement: "War is minutes of terror surrounded by weeks of boredom." It takes courage to respond during the minutes of terror, but it also takes courage to maintain during the weeks of boredom. When I think of men like Jim, I realize that they were successful because they were courageous—not courageous because they were successful. It took courage to run into the exploding guns of the enemy, and it took courage to keep your mind on your mission when all you had to do was sit around cleaning your gun and counting your ammunition. A soldier's inner calm came, therefore, not from the outcome of the battle, but from his ability to maintain courage.

Calm in the workplace requires the same factor as calm on the battlefield. Those who choose to be courageous are those who are going to enjoy inner rest at their jobs. Courageous people are those who subordinate their fears to the task before them. They don't let the heat and anger of the battle distract them from their ultimate purpose.

With this in mind, let me ask a crucial question: Is it possible to be a success at home *and* at work? I believe it is. But I believe it will only happen if we are willing to be courageous enough to make some daring decisions about our work. Men and women who take these steps of courage can enjoy confidence in the middle of the boredom and calm in the middle of the battle.

Enjoying rest in the work arena requires courage in four areas. Let's examine them together.

Courage to Reject the World's View of Success

Changing the way we view success is imperative if a person wants to enjoy rest at work.

If we go by the "system's" view, success is determined by achievement and rewards. Self-help books and motivational speakers preach the gospel of visualization or the philosophy of "dream it today—claim it tomorrow." Success becomes a goal that is measured in status, recognition, or dollar signs. This is based on the belief that inner needs can be satisfied with things—that success is wrapped up in what you gain. If you accept this line of thinking you will *absolutely* be denied a sense of calm and rest in your heart. Restlessness will spill over into your marriage, your children, and your health. It will do more damage than any of your accomplishments could offset.

There is probably no other way for me to state my feelings on this matter than in a bold, sweeping way. So here goes . . .

SUCCESS SHOULD *NEVER* BE PURSUED AS A GOAL. IF YOU MAKE SUCCESS YOUR GOAL, YOU ARE SETTING YOURSELF UP FOR DISAPPOINTMENT.

Is that strong enough? It isn't the message of the environment in which we work, but it is advice that, if taken, will save you years of restlessness. Why am I so bold about this? Because I believe the American family has been fed a lie, and American business has been victimized in the process. When success is defined in dollar signs and then encouraged to become a goal, a person's motivations go through radical and damaging transformation.

"Things" become the object of our affections. People become commodities to be used. Playing becomes subordinate to winning. Absolute rules become relative guidelines. And individuals end up worshiping themselves. This is the theology of the success fantasy. When success is our goal, we can never be satisfied.

That's because success was never *meant* to be a goal. It was meant to be an *outcome* of certain qualities and wise priorities. Qualities such as hard work, rendering a good service and product for a fair price, backing up your work, and maintaining integrity all the way—these are the things that bring success. These types of qualities allow room for us to be human. To be as good as we can, but maybe not as good as the next guy. People who work hard and fair can accept their shortcomings and inevitable failures—because success for them is an outcome, not a goal. It's a process, not a product.

It's what you are, not what you do.

I ran across an excellent article by Eugene Peterson that looks at two key players from the New Testament. How he evaluated success by studying these two men presents a fresh angle on the subject.

Among the apostles, the one absolutely stunning success was Judas, and the one thoroughly groveling failure was Peter. Judas was a success in the ways that most impress us: he was successful both financially and politically. He cleverly arranged to control the money of the apostolic band; he skillfully manipulated the political forces of the day to accomplish his goal. And Peter was a failure in ways that we most dread: he was impotent in a crisis and socially inept. At the arrest of Jesus he collapsed, a hapless, blustering coward; in the most critical situations of his life with Jesus, the confession on the road to Caesarea Philippi and the vision on the Mount of transfiguration, he said the most embarrassingly inappropriate things. He was not the companion we would want with us in time of danger, and he was not the kind of person we would feel comfortable with at a social occasion.

Time, of course, has reversed our judgments on the two men. Judas is now a byword for betrayal, and Peter is one of the most honored names in the church and in the world. Judas is a villain; Peter is a saint. Yet the world continues to chase after the successes of Judas, financial wealth and political power, and to defend itself against the failures of Peter, impotence and ineptness.[16]

If Peter had been employed at the same company as my frustrated friend in Texas, he would have spent a lot of time working at the card table and making appointments from the pay phone. But he would still have been one of the greatest success stories in the office.

That's because *success* is *significance*. It's knowing that your value comes from God and doesn't need achievement and rewards in order to be realized. Knowing that God loved you enough to save you, forgive you, and guarantee your eternal destiny gives you the significance to be a success. It frees you up to use work as a vehicle to facilitate your family rather than a force that holds them hostage.

SUCCESS
THE ART OF MAXIMIZING THE MARKETPLACE
IN ORDER TO SERVE YOUR HIGHER CALLING
AS A FAMILY MEMBER

Let's stop a minute and do a mental inventory. How do you define success? Are you deriving your sense of worth and value from your accomplishments at work? Do you gauge the level of your success as a person by the lifestyle that you enjoy? Could you be content even if you knew that you could never move beyond your present status at work?

I have a hard time being objective on these questions myself. Maybe it would help if you asked your spouse or your children how *they* think you would answer.

We need to be courageous enough to disagree with the world's view of success. We might take some criticism, and we might not advance as quickly, but we can maintain rest in the middle of a work arena intoxicated with getting ahead.

Courage to Accept a Level of Satisfaction

A common thread that runs through the lives of people who enjoy rest in the marketplace is the ability to be satisfied with their current lifestyle. This takes even more courage than changing one's view of success, and runs directly counter to everything the world teaches.

Most people's income increases as they get older. Cost of living and inflation may make the net increase a minus, but the wage or salary usually goes up. There is nothing wrong with raising your standard of living as your income goes up, but somewhere along the way it's vital to hit a level of satisfaction. Those who discipline themselves to do this find their work more fulfilling—because the money that is being made from the work can go toward other worthwhile things. It also allows you to appreciate and maintain your home and possessions because they must now serve you for a longer period of time.

It takes courage for a couple to set a standard of living as a goal and then to be satisfied once they reach it. The world of consumption and indulgence would consider this foolish. But the family who wants to share the gift of rest must be able to put a lid on their "wants."

I have an attorney friend who bought a piece of land in an exclusive area of his midwestern town. His plans were to build on it once his ship came in. After winning a couple of landmark cases, his ship came in, docked, and was ready to be unloaded. I saw him a few months after he had received his commissions for his work. I asked if he had started construction on his house.

I was impressed with his answer. He told me that he and his wife decided their current neighborhood was a good place to live. Their children's friends were there and the kids were enjoying their schools. They decided to add on to their present house and make it their long-term home. He was excited because it left them abundant resources to support the Lord's work and share with unfortunate people.

There seems to be a direct relationship between a person's heart and his checkbook. When a couple decide to settle for a certain standard, and stop chasing the Joneses all over town, they experience a rest in their work and in their home that no higher standard of living could supply.

It takes courage to make the choice to be satisfied.

It takes courage to invest the excess in others when you could be indulging yourself.

It takes courage to say no to wants that would only complicate your life.

But the reward of inner rest is worth it.

Courage to Maintain Rules of Good Stewardship

A lot of people defraud themselves of rest at work because they have refused to live within their means. They get mad at their job for not making them "enough money." They find themselves studying the paper for better job offers and doing a lot of interviews. The problem is that a higher paying job won't solve the problem.

It's easy to make a joke about it: "I'm not overdrawn, I'm undercapitalized!" Either way, it's a restless nightmare. It's humiliating to always have to be looking over your shoulder. But debt keeps you that way. And it spoils the joy you could be receiving from work.

People who struggle with living within their means follow a similar pattern—they neglect their needs to satisfy their wants.

> They've got a new car, but are behind on the rent.

> They can't afford to take their baby in for a check-up, but can afford cable TV.

> They can't afford braces for their kids' teeth, but can afford to go to the lake regularly to play with their boat.

> They can't afford to save, but they can afford to eat out regularly.

It takes courage to admit that you may be holding your family hostage by poor stewardship. It takes courage to get out of debt. It takes courage to stay out of debt. But those who are willing to face this area and do something about it are in the best position to bring rest to their work.

It doesn't matter whether we live on a fixed income or an open-ended bonus, a wage or a draw, all families are better off on a budget.

A good budget provides for: payment of bills for necessities (food, clothing, shelter); investment in now (entertainment or "wants"); investment in the future (savings); and investment in eternity (giving to God's work in the world).

If you have to cut, you start with the entertainment and "wants" section. Once again, that takes courage. It flies in the face of the average person's programming and desires. But those who exercise strong-minded determination in this area of their lives get to reap the reward of going to work without a gun to their head.

No statement on finding rest *in* your work would be complete without a reminder to find rest *from* your work. God's Word doesn't leave this principle open for debate. The Bible is outspoken on the subject of taking a day off. God established it as a pattern when He created the earth.

> Thus the heavens and the earth were completed, and all their hosts. And by the seventh day God completed His work which He had done; and He rested on the seventh day from all His work which He had done. Then God blessed the seventh day and sanctified it, because in it He rested from all His work which God had created and made (Genesis 2:1-3).

After God established the pattern, He established the law of the Sabbath.

> Remember the sabbath day to keep it holy. Six days you shall labor and do all your work, but the seventh day is a sabbath of the LORD your God; in it you shall not do any work . . . For in six days the LORD made the heavens and the earth, the sea and all that is in them, and rested on the seventh day; therefore the LORD blessed the sabbath day and made it holy (Exodus 20:8-11).

Workaholism may be applauded by the corporate structure and may provide the surest route "to the top," but God says it's wrong. He wants us to observe a day off. Our brain needs it, our body needs it, our spirit needs it, and our family needs it. It's a commandment designed to make us more effective and useful to the people we are called to serve.

Courage to Sacrifice the Now for the Forever

The man I spoke of at the opening of this chapter wanted solutions to his frustration. He didn't want to remain working from the card table in the corner, but he wasn't sure that he or his family could take the pressure that went with the key to the salesman of the month's office, either. He was about to overdose on *Tums* because of the stress that his job had brought him.

The answer for him is the answer for a lot of people. He had to muster up the courage to sacrifice. What he ended up having to do was sacrifice his standard of living. He and his wife decided that while being in last place wasn't acceptable, being in first place simply carried too high a price tag. The demands that first place required were directly at the expense of the time needed by his children. So he chose a path that gave him adequate income—though not as much as he was used to. By cutting out some of the extras in his life, he learned a good lesson about contentment.

I love stories with happy endings, don't you?

Is there a happy ending for your story too?

It all depends on your choices. You may be needing the courage to sacrifice in order to bring a sense of rest and contentment back into your job. People prepared to make the hard decisions stand to win the most in life.

You may not be qualified for your job. Pray for the courage to admit it.

You may not be trained for your job. Develop a strategy to get the help you need.

You may not make enough money. Be prepared to cut your spending until you can get a raise or a higher paying job.

You may not be conscientious at your job. Have the courage to confess it as a sin against yourself, your family, and your employer.

You may not like your job. Endure it as a necessity for the income of your family until you can get something better.

We all need the courage to be honest with ourselves about our work. We need to keep in mind that it is a vehicle to accommodate the people whom we love. It is an opportunity to make a contribution and receive fair compensation. But if it becomes a consuming god that we worship or a dreaded nuisance that we neglect, it will drain us of the rest that it could have offered. Work is a privilege and a responsibility.

Charles Kingsley put it this way:

> Thank God every morning when you get up that you have something to do which must be done, whether you like it or not. Being forced to work, and forced to your best, will breed in you temperance and self-control, diligence and strength of will, cheerfulness and contentment, and a hundred virtues which the idle never know.[17]

CHAPTER 13

Gaining Rest in Your Relationships

MY town's nickname is "The Valley of the Sun."
Phoenix is an oasis in the middle of the arid Arizona desert. The mountains that rise up out of the desert floor present a stark and haunting beauty to the skyline. They also present a temptation.

There is something about a mountain that brings out the ego in people. We see it and we just have to conquer it. It has something to do with it "being there." Mountains are nature's giants—its Goliaths. Men get this strange craving to dominate them.

We have our share of men and women who take on our mountains. For those who want to do it the easy way (like me), we have well-kept paths with rest stops along the way. But there are always the daring and adventurous who want to make their own path. They study the mountain and try to figure out the worst way to go from the bottom to the top, and then take off.

I've learned something about the mountains in our valley. They're not very merciful. They have a special way of showing their temper with those people who choose to challenge their more treacherous surfaces. The cactus, scorpions, and rattlesnakes are the lesser of the obstacles. The worst threat is the mountain itself.

Camelback Mountain lies on the east side of the valley. Its silhouette is true to its name. This gigantic "sleeping camel" looks appropriate resting in the middle of our desert. But even though it *appears* to be sleeping, it holds a lot of lively surprises to anyone thinking they can slip up its back.

Creased behind the right "ear" of Camelback Mountain is Echo Canyon. It is a deep cutaway that tempts a lot of hikers and mountain climbers. Its cliffs are hard for them to pass up.

One of the rare times that I was back in this canyon, an accident occurred. A climber had tried to scale the cliff and lost his footing. He dropped quite a ways before a stone tooth sticking out from the cliff caught his body. I wasn't very close to the scene of the accident, but from my vantage point I could see a small group of people leaning out over a ledge and looking down. Their animated movements made it obvious that someone had fallen.

Search and rescue people were summoned, and Air-Evac waited in the wings. It took a while for the experienced team of rescuers to arrive. It took even longer for them to get what they came for.

Because of where the climber fell, and the extent of his injuries, it was impossible to simply lower someone down on the end of a rope and bring him up. It was impossible for the helicopter to descend between the narrow cliffs.

I watched from binoculars as men spoke into their walkie-talkies. I don't know who they were talking to, but in about ten minutes a helicopter came up from the other side of the mountain and hovered over them. It lowered its package in a few seconds and then flew away. The men tore open the package and started assembling something from the materials inside.

From the look of it, they had done this before. In a few brief minutes, a rescue platform was hovering over the side of the cliff. Cables had been nailed into the rock, and the tiny scaffolding beneath it had been anchored.

Within seconds after the platform was secured, men were rappelling off its side. A rescue basket followed them down from cables hooked to the edge. The men disappeared briefly. I knew they had the fallen climber when the men still on top started cranking up the basket. By the time the basket cleared the edge of the cliff, Air-Evac was hovering over top. They hoisted the fallen man onto the platform and in the same motion connected him to the hook that had been lowered from the helicopter. About ten seconds later this injured climber was inside the airborne hospital racing to the nearest emergency room.

A fallen climber. It sounds like a contradiction. In reality, the two words go together—they are inseparable. Every climber who starts up the side of a mountain realizes that falling is a risk of climbing. He may fear the inevitable fall, and do everything within his power to avoid it, but he can't eliminate the possibility of it if he is committed to the climb.

SCALING THE FUTURE

As the clock pulls the twenty-first century closer, we realize that it is going to be a century of challenge and change like nothing we have ever experienced before. This new century looms out in the distant like a great mountain. It is overwhelming and threatening to those who don't like challenges. It can be intimidating to those who don't look forward to change.

But it is coming.

A lot of people have reason to be threatened by the presence of something as massive as a new century. We'd like to live life one day at a time, but the sophistication of the Age of Information won't allow it. Like it or not, the future is a force to be reckoned with, and those who want to take it one day at a time are probably going to be the ones who have the most problem with it.

That's because the future, like the mountains that surround my home, is not going to be very merciful to inexperienced, casual climbers. It's going to be tough enough on those who know what they are doing. This is the very nature of change. Changing times are surprising times, and one thing that people climbing mountains don't want are surprises.

We are not going to be able to go around the future. We may desire to stay camped at its base—stuck in the past. But that will probably not work. We've learned from history that those who fight progress seldom win. Progress has a way of bulldozing over those who want to hang on to yesterday.

Like it or not, the future is coming. The best way to deal with it is to plan on making the climb.

Personally, that thought gets me very excited. I don't want to stay camped in the past. The future might represent challenge and change, but it also holds many great opportunities. The vistas we will see as we climb to the future are going to offer us more perspective than we've ever had before. The mountain of the future is filled with secrets, but they will become our new discoveries. Those discoveries are going to bring new challenges and opportunities for the resourceful and industrious people who embrace them.

But good and bad follow each other around. The future will also offer new threats to the family, new competition for marriages, and new anxiety for the restless spirit of man. That's why we can't plan on scaling it alone.

You've Got a Friend

If we want to make it through the future in one piece, we're going to need some help. The pressures of change are going to make it more difficult to solo. We

are going to have to team up as a couple and as a family—
closer than ever before. But we're going to need more
than that. We'll need a network of people surrounding
us and helping us as we make our way. This network of
support so vital for the future is the same network we
need so desperately in the present. If we ever expect to
negotiate the treacherous climb of the future, we are
going to have to establish a strong climbing team now.

Two groups make up this team—friends . . . and the
church. Both are necessary. The family who has friends
and the family who has a church is the family who doesn't
need to fear what is coming.

Friends and the church satisfy two crucial needs in
our life. First of all, they provide *support*. They are helping
hands and strong arms that help pull us over the rough
spots. They are the ones who serve as our search and
rescue team when we fall. They join us in celebrating
our victories and share tears with us in our sorrow.

The second crucial need that friends and church
satisfy is *accountability*. They help hold us on the path.
They become the "caution" signs and guardrails that
keep us out of danger. Support and accountability are
crucial needs for the family pressured by the demands
of life.

When I was watching the search and rescue team
recover the man who had fallen off of Camelback Mountain, I was impressed with how well they knew their job.
If amateurs would have attempted the rescue, the man's
life might have been in greater jeopardy. But even the
rescue team was limited. They needed equipment and
resources to perform their task. The helicopters, the
strong platform, and the climbing equipment set them
free to do their work thoroughly.

We need friends, but we also need the equipment—
the platform—to help us when we're down. The church
provides that well-anchored rescue platform. It is that
visible structure anchored on the Rock that cannot be
shaken.

But what if the equipment wasn't maintained? What if the cables were defective and the steel rods of the platform weak? What if the men didn't know what they were doing? Because amateurs can masquerade as professionals and faulty equipment can look good on the surface, we need to be careful. Friends will occasionally be called on to help us through tough times. We have to make sure that we have tough friends. Churches can look great on the outside, but can they serve as the platform of strength and provide the barriers of protection that we so desperately need?

If we want to maintain rest as we scale the mountain peaks of change and uncertainty, we need competent friends and a responsible church. These aren't impossible to find. We just need to know what we're looking for.

THE PROFILE OF A GOOD FRIEND

Friendships are maintained at different levels of commitment. They run the gamut from casual, fair-weather friends to loving, intimate friends. Most people have a large group of friends who fall into the first category and only a handful (maybe only one) who fall into the second category. When you fall down or get lost in your climb through the crags and cliffs of life, it doesn't matter how many casual friends you have. It only matters that you have someone you would consider a true and loving friend.

Loving friends are the people who come to your mind when you're confused and need advice . . . when you're worried and in need . . . when you receive good news and just have to tell someone. They are the first ones on your guest list, the first choice for an evening out. They're the ones you would trust with your possessions, your kids, your life. Their job is a big one. Over the period of a lifetime they must serve as confidant, counselor, referee, prophet, and pallbearer.

If you can only claim one such person in your lifetime, you are rich.

Because they play such a key part in our lives we must choose them carefully and cultivate them regularly. But not knowing what to look for sends a lot of people off course in their search for good friends. We can easily get sidetracked when we look for characteristics like compatibility, common interest, and personality. These things are important, but they are not the kind of characteristics that can help us through our hurts.

If I'm going to be taking risks as I climb the mountains that rise up out of my circumstances and experiences, I want a couple of people around me who have three qualities. My observation is that those who have these three qualities can be your greatest source of genuine rest outside of your family.

Loyalty

None of us want to be put on hold when we call on our friends. We need to know they are going to be there when we need them.

Loyal friends assume the best about us. They defend us when we are accused. They stand by our side when we are guilty and help us endure our shame.

One of my closest friends is a man I don't get to see very often. Mike is the proprietor of my favorite antique store in Phoenix. We've enjoyed a lot of laughs and discussed a lot of hurts. I've always felt that Mike would never desert me in times of trouble. That's because he understands loyalty. If I did something horrible— shamed my family and my reputation—most people would turn away from me. I've always felt, however, that Mike's the kind of guy who would never turn his back. If I ever went to prison, he would visit me.

I'm fortunate to have several friends like Mike. They are loyal in good times and bad. For obvious reasons I don't plan to put their loyalty to the test. But it's nice to know they have this quality if I ever need it.

Honesty

Good friends must be honest. It's an extremely rare quality in a friend. It's hard to find because we don't encourage our friends to exercise it in our lives. But if I want to make it through the climb, I need friends who will be straightforward, candid, and sincere.

Proverbs 27:6 is one of those verses that you wish wasn't in the Bible, but after you've felt its truth are glad that it is. It says, "Faithful are the wounds of a friend, but deceitful are the kisses of an enemy."

Accountability is painful. There comes a time in all of our lives when we need the truth that hurts. None of us like to be confronted when we're wrong, but fortunate is the man or woman who has a friend who loves enough to risk rejection . . . and tell the truth anyway.

A friend who is willing to lay friendship on the line to tell us the truth is rare. We need to encourage the people close to us to not be timid about pointing out the danger areas during our climb. We don't need to get defensive if they point out that we are using poor climbing techniques. Their honesty may save us a lot of pain.

Sensitivity

A third quality of a good friend is a genuine sensitivity to our needs and feelings. They need to recognize that our feelings, our secrets, and our hopes are treasures that must be guarded.

A sensitive person knows when a joke has gone too far. He has a way of recognizing when our frustrations are hitting the kindling point. He gets good at knowing when to get close and when to give us room. His caution with privileged information assures that our secrets are safe with him.

Very few people get straight A's on their friendship report card. On the subjects of loyalty, honesty, and sensitivity, the best friend you have may only maintain a C average. Don't panic. Good friendships don't just happen. They are deliberately planned and developed over a lifetime.

The best way to get good friends is to *be* a good friend.

People who develop the qualities of loyalty, honesty, and sensitivity in their lives stand a better chance of attracting friends that have these qualities too.

The best mountain climbers in the world seek each other out. If they are going to take on the biggest challenges, they want to do it with the best team. Whether we are scaling the cliffs that surround us in the present or the mountains of change that loom in the future, we need good friends on our climbing team. They will help keep our hearts at rest when our lives have to hang over the edge.

The Profile of a Good Church

If we must climb our way through today and over tomorrow, we need more than a few friends. We need competent coaching, accurate maps, and reliable equipment. Going forward in life requires us to face a myriad of unknowns. The church can help provide the things we need to face these unknowns.

The church is an extended family. It is an organism made up of a lot of families with common goals.

But a pretty building and a steeple do not mean that a church is equipped to equip. Churches are like people; some know what they're doing and some don't. Choosing a good church is crucial.

There are no perfect churches, just as there are no perfect friends. If something is going to be made up of people, it is going to have problems. Churches are families. Families have problems. But there are criteria which I believe can be used as a yardstick. A good church should be able to measure up in each area.

For our discussion, let's call these criteria the "focus points" of the church. Although I will not list all that I consider important, I feel that the three I do list will give you the best chance of finding a church that can help you maintain rest in your soul.

A Focus on the LORD

That point, you say, should go without saying. Unfortunately, many churches with a cross on their roof and Christ in their stained glass window have little to do with either. God's Spirit has no influence upon them.

These types of churches are more like religious country clubs. They meet social needs and physical needs, but they don't meet spiritual needs.

My conviction is that a church cannot equip us for the climb if it cannot bring us to God. I also maintain the conviction that if a church wants to bring us to God, it must ultimately take us down a path that leads to the foot of the cross. In other words, it isn't God in general, but Jesus in particular that we need.

Before we place our family under the authority of a church, we must be certain that the church is under the authority of God. Listen next Sunday to the sermon. It won't be hard to determine if your church is focused on the Lord.

A Focus on the Scriptures

A church that can deliver rest to a human heart must speak and operate from the authority of Scripture. God didn't leave us in the dark. He gave us clear instructions.

The last half of the twentieth century has been a difficult time for the church. Men who have only been around a few decades have concluded that the Bible, which has been around for a few millennia, is not relevant today. Many of these men stand in ornate pulpits throughout our country. The Bible is not the subject of their sermons, but the object of their ridicule.

When I deal with people who go to churches that do not respect the Word of God, I pick up an insecurity in them that runs deep. They are starving for rest because they have been denied Truth. When we go to church, we don't want sermons and teaching based strictly on opinions. We need truth that jumps from every page of the Bible.

A church that facilitates rest, then, is a church that focuses on the Lord Jesus and focuses on His truth.

A Focus on the Family

Churches committed to helping us on our climb through the canyons of time must have a focus on the parent/child dynamic that makes up the foundation of our culture. As parents, we need all the help we can get. Our children need instruction that reinforces our values.

A church committed to the family recognizes its responsibility. It must be an ally to the parent and an asset to the home. It must recognize its calling to bring order and calm to a confusing world.

Good churches enfold the hurting and the helpless. They are a haven for the hurried and a guiding light to the confused. They offer their love to the outcast, their encouragement to the single parent, and their sensitive rebuke to those who are walking too close to the sheer cliffs and dangerous drop-offs of twentieth-century living.

Sundays can be the highlight of a family's week if they have the privilege of being part of a church with proper priorities. Restless hearts need the church. Outside of our immediate family, the church is the only organization that will commit to seeing us into the world, helping us through life, and standing by our side as we slip into the beyond.

CLIMB EVERY MOUNTAIN

It's possible to maintain a calm and confident heart as we climb the mountains ahead. The right friends and the right path are all that we need. We can anticipate a few surprises, we can count on a few stumbles, we may even find that falling over the edge a time or two is unavoidable. But the right people with the right rescue equipment can make it all bearable.

We need not fear the mountains of change; they are ours to climb. From their pinnacles we will gain new perspective on the life God has called us to live.

EPILOGUE

SEVERAL summers ago the air traffic controllers union and the White House decided to play tug-of-war. I was one of the millions of airline travelers who served as rope for the tug. The tickets for my trips only served to prove that I had, at one time, been guaranteed a seat on a flight. Flights were being canceled by the minute. The only laws that were still in force were the laws of aerodynamics. But it was hard to find a plane on which you could experience them.

That's what caused me to arrive late into a Michigan airport. The pastor picking me up was a warm, sensitive man. But he wasn't good at flexibility. A large group of teenagers were assembling at a camp in central Michigan, and I was supposed to be there with them at that very moment.

That's how I found myself rocketing down the interstate in a subcompact—moving considerably faster than a respectable preacher's car ought to travel. We headed north on a freeway that cuts up the middle of the state—

the immediate countryside little more than a green blur out my window. Gripped by hurry and worry my driver bent over the wheel with set jaw and clenched teeth. My own relaxed demeanor probably infuriated him. But why get excited? I'd long since learned that when you're working with teenagers, the schedule should be written in pencil.

My companion, however, still viewed the "program" as some immutably perfect plan. He couldn't imagine such a thing as adapting to imposed changes.

As he drove and worried, I sat back to enjoy the ride and maybe get some rest. The problem was he wouldn't slow down. When we passed the Porsche, *I* started to get nervous.

Then something caught my eye in the distance as we screamed north along the freeway. Even at that speed, you couldn't miss it. It was so tall and distinct you could see it for over a mile.

It was a cross.

I've seen bold statements about the Christian faith placed in strategic visible locations before. The people who put them there have good intentions, but most of them come off as too imposing for my evangelistic tastes. But being a Christian, I naturally wanted to read the message printed across the horizontal beam of the cross. As we passed by, I saw that the message was not for evangelistic purposes as much as it was to direct people to an out-of-the-way attraction.

The message read: SEE WHERE THE HYMN "OLD RUGGED CROSS" WAS WRITTEN.

The narrow road that stretched off into the country looked lonely and untraveled.

I asked my worried driver about the sign. He remarked that he had observed it before but had never bothered to see where it led. But we had people waiting and messages to communicate, so we hastened on.

A couple of exits north we pulled off the highway and drifted through a small town. Just about a mile or so farther we came to the camp where I would be speaking all week. The kids were having a great time. They seemed oblivious to the fact that circumstances weren't cooperating with people's self-made plans.

We assembled them in the chapel, the program began, I spoke, and my ministerial chauffeur began to relax. I even caught him smiling. By the next morning, summer camp was back on schedule.

As I was going through the motions of my responsibilities as "Camp Pastor," I found my mind slipping down the freeway a few exits. *See Where the Hymn "Old Rugged Cross" Was Written*, kept surfacing in my thoughts. Maybe it was my interest in the past or my natural curiosity toward out-of-the-way corners of life, but I felt that I couldn't afford to be this close and not go the extra mile to see what this message on the freeway was all about.

After morning chapel on Thursday, I grabbed a hymnbook and obtained permission from the camp manager to borrow a camp vehicle. In about ten minutes I was heading out on the dirt road in search of the cross.

If you've ever worked with camps, then you know that "camp vehicles" seldom meet the dictionary definition for transportation. I was in a pickup truck. It wasn't very old, but it was already a piece of junk. I had a feeling that the best miles had been driven out of it by some member of a church, and then it was "donated to the Lord's service" at the point when the value of the tax deduction was greater than the value of the trade-in. It felt like it was held together by wire and tape, and it steered like a sled. The radio had a bad connection so I decided I'd have to miss the opportunity of listening to the local country and western station.

Instead, I hummed the tune to the song whose title had been painted on that distinct sign that had caught my attention. In less than an instant I found myself heart-deep in nostalgia.

You know how it is. You hear a song you haven't heard for a long time, and something sends the circuits in your brain sifting through the seldom used files of your memory. Certain songs mysteriously attach themselves to places or people in your past. Just a few notes is all it takes to fill you with bittersweet, half-remembered emotions.

I found myself back in Pennsylvania, standing in church, sharing a hymnbook with Mom and Dad. Singing those redemptive words . . .

On a hill far away . . .

I knew all the words before I could read. The hymn was one of the standards, the classics that anyone who went to a Protestant church would know.

I pulled off of the highway and headed east through the rolling Michigan countryside. I came on a small village that looked like it hadn't changed much in fifty years. It had an anemic look to it. The buildings needed painting, the streets were cluttered, and the people looked bored.

I kept following the road, expecting to see little signs leading the way. There was nothing. Just country road and countryside. After a couple of miles of wandering around, I decided to double-back to the little town and see if I could get some help.

A man who looked as if he worked hard for a living was the first person I saw. I slowed down and got his attention with my question. He knew the place I was looking for and gave me a few directions.

You know how it is when you develop a mental picture of something that predetermines what you think you'll find, only to find yourself disappointed when you get there? I'd been picturing a little frame house with a few rooms and some antique furniture. I figured there'd be some photos of the songwriter and a history of his life.

All I found was a simple cross by a half-circled drive-way that looped off of the isolated road. The sign on the cross conveyed the message that George Bennard had lived on this site, and it was here that he wrote the hymn that would become an inspiration to millions of people for generations to come.

I climbed out of the truck and walked out onto the grass by the side of the driveway. I was standing on the top of a slight hill. It was raised just enough to give a good view of the landscape. I walked out about a hundred feet from the truck to take in the view. When I turned around to walk back, I noticed a faint outline in the grass. The shadow of the cross fell across the lines of the old foundation upon which Mr. Bennard's house had been built.

The house was gone. Only the cross was standing.

Retrieving the hymnal from the pickup, I walked to where I figured the walls of this little house must have stood. I sat down in the grass, looked up the hymn in the index, and leafed through to the appropriate page.

The editor of the hymnal indicated that Mr. Bennard had written the song in 1913. I thought to myself that life had certainly changed since he had put his poem of hope to music. We were looping the moon while he lived in an era when aviation was barely out of the cradle.

I was glad that I had paid attention in history class, because my mind started clicking out information that made me rethink my original contrast of times. When George Bennard sat in this house composing his beautiful hymn, his world was exploding with technology and information. Automobiles, electric lights, telephones, and phonograraghs were already making their alterations to the way people thought. A few months after he penned his hymn, young men from all over the world would put on their uniforms and meet in the trenches of Europe to fight the "War to end all Wars." Some of them would come from the very towns through which I had driven that morning. The League of Nations, the United Nations, and scores of other alliances would attempt and fail to maintain the peace these men fought for. World War I would be a costly dress rehearsal for World War II and the unending conflicts that have followed it to the present day.

Mr. George Bennard was a part of the generation of people who began the maddening marathon that our generation still runs. He was feeling the pressure of rapid change just like we do, and he took comfort in the permanence and hope of a bloodstained cross erected almost two thousand years ago. The inspiration that helped him write his song in the first part of the twentieth century was still working in the heart of a man sitting in his backyard seventy years later.

I set the open hymnal down in the grass and began to sing the words out loud.

> On a hill far away stood an old rugged cross
> The emblem of suffering and shame.
> And I love that old cross where the Dearest and Best
> For a world of lost sinners was slain.
>
> So I'll cherish the old rugged cross,
> Till my trophies at last I lay down;
> I will cling to the old rugged cross,
> And exchange it some day for a crown.

Although I could never forget the first stanza to this song, I was glad I'd brought the hymnal with me. I needed those other stanzas to complete the impression of that moment on my hurried heart. I thought of George Bennard sitting at a little desk looking out his window. A confidence in his heart allowed him to look beyond the hills of Michigan to a hill outside of Jerusalem and the cross that was built for the God-who-became-a-man.

O that old rugged cross, so despised by the world,
Has a wondrous attraction for me;
For the dear Lamb of God left His glory above
To bear it to dark Calvary.

In the old rugged cross, stained with blood so divine,
A wondrous beauty I see;
For t'was on that old cross Jesus suffered and died
To pardon and sanctify me.

To that old rugged cross I will ever be true,
Its shame and reproach gladly bear;
Then He'll call me someday to my home faraway,
Where His glory forever I'll share.[18]

A cross . . . by a freeway. It seems a fitting conclusion
to our study of hurried lifestyles.

The title of this book, *Little House on the Freeway*, was
an intentional play on words. "Little House" reminds us
of a long ago era of tranquillity and rest. The "Freeway"
is a like-it-or-not statement of where we are . . . and a
promise of where we're going.

It's the symbol of a life that moves too fast.

But we've got to keep going. We can't go back. And
you know, I really wouldn't want to even if I could. The
future holds too many exciting possibilities, too many
intriguing opportunities.

But along our high-speed journey, a simple cross
calls us to pull over, to take a side trip few people seem
to have time for. They've got schedules and deadlines,
goals and objectives. The "program" looms large, and
detours don't fit the itinerary.

Those who do make the journey find lonely back-
roads and people who don't seem to fit the "dress for
success" mentality.

Sometimes they're disappointed with their initial
visit. They expect to find the comfort of man-made
shrines and the mementos of human accomplishments.

Yet the memories of men crumble all too soon, leaving only the distinct silhouette of the timeless, ageless cross.

The signs pointing the way to the cross won't be neon-lit and three feet high. If you're not watching, you could drive right by. But those who slow down long enough to negotiate the turn and make the side trip to a backroad in Palestine have a promise waiting for them from the Lord of the cross:

> You will seek Me and find Me, when you search for Me with all your heart (Jeremiah 29:13).

APPENDIX

101 Ways to Give Rest to Your Family

B ECOMING good at the things that build inner confidence and calm takes practice—and a dash of creativity! The following list might provide some cloud-seeding for a brainstorm or two of your own. Have some fun with your family . . . and get ready for a good rest.

1. Pay off your credit cards.
2. Take off ten pounds or accept where you are without any more complaints.
3. Eat dinner together as a family for seven days in a row.
4. Take your wife on a dialogue date (no movie, guys).
5. Read your kids a classic book (Twain's a good start).
6. Memorize the Twenty-third Psalm as a family.
7. Give each family member a hug for twenty-one days in a row (that's how long the experts say it takes to develop a habit).
8. Pick a night of the week in which the television will remain unplugged.
9. Go out for a non-fast-food dinner as a family.
10. Pray for your spouse and children every day.
11. Plan a vacation together.
12. Take a vacation together.

13. Read a chapter from the Bible every day until it becomes a habit.
14. Sit together as a family in church.
15. Surprise your teenager. Wash his car and fill up his gas tank.
16. Take an afternoon off from work; surprise your child by excusing him from school and taking him to a ball game.
17. Take a few hours one afternoon and go to the library as a family.
18. Take a walk as a family.
19. Write each member of your family a letter sharing why you value them.
20. Give your spouse a weekend getaway with a friend (same gender!) to a place of their choice.
21. Go camping as a family.
22. Go to bed early (one hour before your normal bedtime) every day for a week.
23. Take each of your children out to breakfast (individually) at least once a month for a year.
24. Turn down a promotion that would demand more time from your family than you can afford to give.
25. Religiously wear your seat belts.
26. Get a complete physical.
27. Exercise a little every day for a month.
28. Make sure you have adequate life insurance on both you and your spouse.
29. Write out information about finances, wills, and important business information that your spouse can use to keep things under control in the event of your death.
30. Make sure your family car is safe (tires, brakes, etc.) and get it tuned up.
31. Replace the batteries in your smoke alarm.
32. Put a security system in your house.
33. Attend the parent/teacher meetings of each child as a couple.
34. Help your kids with their homework.
35. Watch the kids on Saturday while your wife goes shopping (but if a friend calls, don't say that you are "babysitting").
36. Explain to your spouse exactly what you do for a living.

37. Put together a picture puzzle. (One thousand pieces or more.)
38. Take time during the week to read a Bible story to your children and then discuss it with them.
39. Encourage each child to submit to you his most perplexing question, and promise him that you'll either answer it or discuss it with him.
40. Finish fixing something around the house.
41. Tell your kids how you and your spouse met.
42. Tell your kids about your first date.
43. Sit down and write your parents a letter thanking them for a specific thing they did for you. (Don't forget to send it!)
44. Go on a shopping spree where you are absolutely committed to buying nothing.
45. Keep a prayer journal for a month. Keep track of the specific ways that God answers your needs.
46. Do some stargazing away from the city with your family. Help your children identify constellations and conclude the evening with prayer to the majestic God who created the heavens.
47. Treat your wife to a beauty make-over (facial, manicure, haircut, etc). I hear they really like this.
48. Give the kids an alternative to watching Saturday morning cartoons (breakfast at McDonald's, garage sales, the park, chores, etc.).
49. Ask your children each day what they did at school (what they learned, who they ate lunch with, etc.).
50. After you make your next major family decision, take your child back through the process and teach him how you arrived at your decision.
51. Start saying to yourself "My car doesn't look so bad."
52. Call your wife or husband from work just to see how they're doing.
53. Compile a family tree and teach your children the history of their ancestors.
54. Walk through an old graveyard with your children.
55. Say no to at least one thing a day—even if it's only a second piece of pie.
56. Write that letter to the network that broadcast the show you felt was inappropriate for prime-time viewing.
57. Turn off the lights and listen to a "praise" tape as you focus your thoughts on the Lord.

58. Write a note to your pastor praising him for something.
59. Take back all the books in your library that actually belong in someone else's library.
60. Give irritating drivers the right to pull in front of you without signaling and yelling at them.
61. Make every effort to not let the sun go down on your anger.
62. Accept legitimate criticism from your wife or a friend without reacting or defending yourself.
63. If your car has a Christian bumper sticker on it—drive like it.
64. Do a Bible study on the "wise man" and the "fool" in Proverbs . . . and then apply what it takes to be wise to your life.
65. Make a list of people who have hurt your feelings over the past year . . . then check your list to see if you've forgiven them.
66. Make a decision to honor your parents, even if they made a career out of dishonoring you.
67. Take your children to the dentist and doctor for your wife.
68. Play charades with your family, but limit subjects to memories from the past.
69. Do the dishes for your wife.
70. Schedule yourself a free day to stay home with your family.
71. Get involved in a family project that serves or helps someone less fortunate.
72. As a family, get involved in a recreational activity.
73. Send your wife flowers.
74. Spend an evening going through old pictures from family vacations.
75. Take a weekend once a year for you and your spouse to get away and renew your relationship.
76. Praise your spouse and children—in their presence—to someone else.
77. Discuss a world or national problem, and ask your children for their opinion on it.
78. Wait up for your teenagers when they are out on dates.
79. Have a "quiet Saturday" (no television, no radio, no stereo . . . no kidding).
80. If your children are little, spend an hour playing with them—but let them determine the game.

81. Have your parents tell your children about life when they were young.
82. Give up soap operas.
83. De-clutter your house.
84. If you have a habit of watching late night television, but have to be to work early every morning, change your habit.
85. Don't accept unnecessary business breakfast appointments.
86. Write missionaries regularly.
87. Go through your closets and give everything that you haven't worn in a year to a clothing relief organization.
88. Become a faithful and frequent visitor of your church's library.
89. Become a monthly supporter of a Third World child.
90. Keep mementos, school projects, awards, etc. of each child in separate files. You'll appreciate these when they've left the nest.
91. Read the biography of a missionary.
92. Give regularly and faithfully to conscientious church endeavors.
93. Place with your will a letter to each family member telling why you were glad you got to share life with him or her.
94. Go through your old records and tapes and discard any of them that might be a bad testimony to your children.
95. Furnish a room (or a corner of a room) with comfortable chairs and declare it the "disagreement corner." When conflicts arise, go to this corner and don't leave until it's resolved.
96. Give each child the freedom to pick his favorite dinner menu at least once a week.
97. Go over to a shut-in's house as a family and completely clean it and get the lawn work done.
98. Call an old friend from your past, just to see how he or she is getting along.
99. Get a good friend to hold you accountable for a specific important need (Bible reading, prayer, spending time with your family, losing a few pounds, etc.).
100. Establish a budget.
101. Go to a Christian marriage enrichment seminar.

NOTES

1. Charles R. Swindoll, *Killing Giants, Pulling Thorns* (Portland, Ore.: Multnomah Press, 1978), p. 79.
2. Andor Foldes, "Beethoven's Kiss," *Reader's Digest*, (November 1986), p. 145.
3. "Crying In the Chapel," by Artie Glenn, Copyright © 1953 by Valley Publishing Inc. Copyright Renewed & Assigned to Unichappell Music, Inc. International Copyright secured. All rights reserved. Used by permission.
4. Rodger Strader, "There Is Peace," © 1982 Belwin-Mills Publishing Corp. International copyright secured Made in USA. All rights reserved. Used by permission.
5. Isaac Watts, "At the Cross."
6. Meg Greenfield, "Why Nothing Is 'Wrong' Anymore," *Newsweek* (July 28, 1986), p. 72.
7. Susanna McBee, "Morality," *U.S. News & World Report* (December 9, 1985), pp. 52-62.
8. "Seasons of a Man." Written by Steve and Annie Chapman. © Copyright 1986 by Dawn Treader Music. All rights reserved. Used by permission of Gaither Copyright Management.
9. Paul Aurandt, *Destiny: From Paul Harvey's "The Rest of the Story"* (New York: Bantam Books, 1983).
10. Calvin Miller, *The Finale* (Downer's Grove, Ill.: InterVarsity Press, 1979).
11. Attributed to Eleanor Roosevelt.
12. John Fischer, "Roses on Wednesday" © 1982 by Word Music (A Div. of Word Inc.) All rights reserved. International copyright Secured. Used by permission.
13. Laurens van der Post and Jane Taylor, *Testament to the Bushmen* (New York: Viking Press, 1984), pp. 130-31.
14. Thomas J. Peters and Nancy Austin, *A Passion for Excellence* (New York: Random House, 1985).
15. David Ogilvy, *Confessions of an Advertising Man* (New York: Atheneum, 1980).
16. Eugene Peterson, "Success or Failure," *Leadership* 4 (Winter 1984): 53.
17. Charles Kingsley, *Leadership* 6 (Summer 1985): 37.
18. "The Old Rugged Cross" Copyright 1913 by George Bennard. © Renewed 1941 by The Rodeheaver Company (A Div. of Word, Inc.) All rights reserved. International copyright secured. Used by permission.

Tim Kimmel is a conference speaker for
GENERATION MINISTRIES
P.O. Box 31031
Phoenix, AZ 85046
(602) 996-9922